COLLINS GEM

German

PHRASE FINDER

HarperCollins*Publishers*

CONSULTANT

Ulrike Seeberger

First published 1993

Copyright © HarperCollins Publishers

Reprint 10 9 8 7 6 5 4 3 2 1

Printed in Great Britain

ISBN 0 00-470284-0

Your *Collins Gem Phrase Finder* is designed to help you locate the exact phrase you need in any situation, whether for holiday or business. If you want to adapt the phrases, we have made sure that you can easily see where to substitute your own words (you can find them in the dictionary section), and the clear, alphabetical, two-colour layout gives you direct access to the different topics.

The *Phrase Finder* includes:

■ Over 70 topics arranged alphabetically from **ACCOMMODATION** to **WORK**. Each phrase is accompanied by a simple pronunciation guide which ensures that there's no problem over pronouncing the foreign words.

■ Practical hints and useful vocabulary highlighted in boxes. Where the English words appear first in the box, this indicates vocabulary you may need. Where the red German words appear first, these are words you are more likely to see written on signs and notices.

WORDS APPEARING IN BLACK ARE ENGLISH WORDS	WORDS APPEARING IN RED ARE GERMAN WORDS

■ Possible phrases you may hear in reply to your questions. The foreign phrases appear in red.

■ A clearly laid-out 5000-word dictionary: English words appear in black and German words appear in red.

■ A basic grammar section which will enable you to build on your phrases.

It's worth spending time before you embark on your travels just looking through the topics to see what is covered and becoming familiar with what might be said to you.

Whatever the situation, your *Phrase Finder* is sure to help!

BUSINESS

ACCOUNTS
BUSINESS—MEETING
COMPUTERS
FAX
IMPORT/EXPORT
LETTERS
OFFICE
WORK

TRAVEL

see CAR
AIR TRAVEL
BOAT & FERRY
BUS
CUSTOMS CONTROL
METRO
TAXI
TRAIN

EATING & DRINKING

DRINKING
EATING OUT
VEGETARIAN
WINES & SPIRITS

CAR

BREAKDOWNS
CAR—DRIVING
CAR—HIRE
CAR—PARTS
PETROL STATION

DIFFICULTIES

COMPLAINTS
EMERGENCIES
PROBLEMS

LEISURE

CELEBRATIONS
CINEMA
ENTERTAINMENT
LEISURE/INTERESTS
MUSIC
SIGHTSEEING & TOURIST OFFICE
SKIING
SPORTS
TELEVISION
THEATRE
WALKING

SHOPPING

CLOTHES
FOOD—GENERAL, FRUIT & VEG.
MAPS, GUIDES & NEWSPAPERS
PHARMACY
PHOTOS & VIDEOS
POST OFFICE
SHOPPING—SHOPS
STATIONERY

ACCOMMODATION

ACCOMMODATION
CAMPING
DISABLED TRAVELLERS
HOTEL
PAYING
ROOM SERVICE
SIGHTSEEING & TOURIST OFFICE

PRACTICALITIES

ALPHABET
BASICS
COLOUR & SHAPE
DAYS, MONTHS & SEASONS
DIRECTIONS
LAUNDRY
LUGGAGE
MEASUREMENTS & QUANTITIES
MONEY
NUMBERS
PAYING
QUESTIONS
REPAIRS
SIGNS & NOTICES
TELEPHONE
TIME—TIME PHRASES

HEALTH

BODY
DENTIST
DOCTOR
EMERGENCIES
PHARMACY

MEETING PEOPLE

BASICS
CELEBRATIONS
GREETINGS
MAKING FRIENDS
WEATHER
WORK

CONTENTS

PRONOUNCING GERMAN ——————— ENGLISH-GERMAN

*Spelling and pronouncing German are easy once you know the basic rules. This book has been designed so that as you read the pronunciation of the phrases you can follow the German. This will help you to recognize the different sounds and you will soon be able to pronounce German from the spelling alone (the stressed syllable is marked in **heavy italics**). Here are a few rules you should know:*

GERMAN	SOUNDS LIKE	EXAMPLE	PRONUNCIATION
■ AU	ow	auto	**ow**to
■ CH	kh	noch	nokh
■ EI	eye	fein	fine
■ IE	ee	sie	zee
■ EU	oy	neun	noyn
■ QU	kv	Quittung	**kvi**-toong
■ S	s	es	es
	z	sie	zee
	sh	sprechen	**shpre**-khen
■ ß	ss	muß	moos
■ U	oo	gut	goot
■ V	f	von	fon
■ W	v	wir	veer
■ UMLAUTS			
■ Ä	eh	hätte	**het**-te
■ ÄU	oy	läutet	**loy**-tet
■ Ö	ur'*	können	**kur'**-nen
■ Ü	oo	grün	groon

A final e is always pronounced, but weakly like the e in the: seide zy-de, bitte bi-te

* ur' as in hurt without the r pronounced

■ ALPHABET

6

*If you haven't booked accommodation in advance, the local tourist office may have a room-booking service – **Zimmervermittlung**.*

ÜBERNACHTUNG MIT FRÜHSTÜCK	BED AND BREAKFAST
ZIMMER FREI / BELEGT	ROOMS AVAILABLE / NO VACANCIES

Do you have a list of accommodation with prices?
Haben Sie eine Liste von Unterkünften mit Preisen?
*hah-ben zee ine-e **lis**-te fon **oon**ter-koonften mit **pri**-zen*

Is there a hotel here?
Gibt es hier ein Hotel?
*gipt es heer ine ho**tel***

Do you have any vacancies?
Haben Sie Zimmer frei?
***hah**-ben zee **tsi**mmer fry*

I'd like (to book) a room
Ich möchte ein Zimmer (buchen)
*ikh mur'kh-te ine **tsi**mmer (**boo**-khen)*

a double room
ein Doppelzimmer
*ine **do**pel-tsimmer*

a single room
ein Einzelzimmer
*ine **ine**-tsel-tsimmer*

with bath
mit Bad
mit baht

with shower
mit Dusche
*mit **doo**-she*

a twin-bedded room
ein Zweibettzimmer
*ine **tsvy**-bet-tsimmer*

a quiet room
ein ruhiges Zimmer
*ine **roo**-hig-es **tsi**mmer*

a room that looks onto the back
ein Zimmer nach hinten
*ine **tsi**mmer nakh **hin**-ten*

with an extra bed for a child
mit einem zusätzlichen Kinderbett
*mit ine-em **tsoo**-sets-likhen **kin**-derbet*

We'd like rooms next to each other
Wir möchten Zimmer nebeneinander
*veer mur'kh-ten **tsi**mmer **nay**ben-ine-ander*

CONT...

We'd like to stay ... nights
Wir möchten ... Nächte bleiben
veer mur'kh-ten ... nekh-te bly-ben

from ... till ...
vom ... bis zum ...
fom ... bis tsoom ...

I will write a letter
Ich schreibe einen Brief
ikh shry-be ine-en breef

I will send a fax
Ich schicke ein Fax
ich shi-ke ine fax

How much is it...?	**per night**	**per week**
Was kostet es...?	pro Nacht	pro Woche
vas kostet es...	*pro nakht*	*pro vo-khe*

How much is...?	**half board**	**full board**
Was kostet...?	Halbpension	Vollpension
vas kostet...	*halp-pen-zyohn*	*folpen-zyohn*

Is breakfast included?
Ist das Frühstück inbegriffen?
ist das froo-shtook in-be-griffen

Have you anything cheaper?
Haben Sie etwas Billigeres?
hah-ben zee etvas bili-ge-res

Can you give us the name of another hotel?
Könnten Sie uns ein anderes Hotel nennen?
kur'n-ten zee oons ine an-de-res hotel ne-nen

■ YOU MAY HEAR

Wir sind ausgebucht
veer sint ows-gebookht
We're full up

Für wieviele Nächte?
foor veefee-le nekh-te
For how many nights?

Wie heißen Sie, bitte?
vee hy-sen zee bi-te
What is your name, please?

Bitte bestätigen Sie...	schriftlich	mit Fax
bi-te be-shtay-tigen zee...	*shrift-likh*	*mit fax*
Please confirm...	by letter	by fax

■ CAMPING ■ HOTEL ■ SIGHTSEEING & TOURIST OFFICE

INVOICE	DIE RECHNUNG
ACCOUNTANT	DER BUCHHALTER / DIE BUCHHALTERIN
TO SETTLE (pay)	BEGLEICHEN

Could I speak to someone in your accounts department?
Könnte ich bitte mit jemand aus der Buchhaltung sprechen?
*kur'n-te ikh **bi**-te mit **yay**mant ows der **bookh**-haltoong **shpre**-khen*

It's regarding your / our invoice number...   **of** (date)...
Es geht um Ihre / unsere Rechnung Nummer...   vom...
*es gayt oom ee-re / **oon**-ze-re **rekh**-noong **noo**mer...   fom...*

I think there is an error
Ich glaube, da liegt ein Irrtum vor
*ikh **glow**-be da leekt ine **ir**-toom for*

The invoice has not been settled yet
Die Rechnung ist noch nicht bezahlt
*dee **rekh**-noong ist nokh nikht be-**tsahlt***

Please supply us with a credit note and new invoice
Bitte schicken Sie uns eine Gutschrift und eine neue Rechnung
*bi-te shicken zee oons ine-e **goot**-shrift oont ine-e **noy**-e **rekh**-noong*

Please address the invoice to...
Bitte schicken Sie die Rechnung an...
*bi-te shicken zee dee **rekh**-noong an...*

The goods should be accompanied by a pro forma invoice
Den Waren sollte eine Proforma-Rechnung beiliegen
*dayn **vah**-ren **zol**-te ine-e pro-forma-rekh-noong **by**-leegen*

Please state content and value of the consignment
Bitte geben Sie Inhalt und Wert der Sendung an
*bi-te gayben zee **in**-halt oont vayrt der **zen**-doong an*

■ NUMBERS ■ TELEPHONE

Most signs are in German and English and you may go through the airport without having to speak any German. Here are a few signs you will find useful to know. Please note that the red and green customs channels no longer apply to EC travellers in Europe.

ANKUNFT	ARRIVALS
PASSKONTROLLE / AUSWEISKONTROLLE	PASSPORT CONTROL
EG - LÄNDER	**EC** PASSPORT HOLDERS
GEPÄCKAUSGABE	BAGGAGE RECLAIM
ZOLL	CUSTOMS CONTROL
EINGANG	ENTRANCE
AUSGANG	EXIT
PARKPLATZ FÜR KURZPARKER	CAR PARK *(short term)*
FLUGHAFENBUS / AIRPORT BUS	SHUTTLE BUS

Where is the luggage for the flight from...?
Wo ist das Gepäck vom Flug aus...?
*vo ist das ge**pek** fom flook ows...*

Where can I change some money?
Wo kann ich hier Geld wechseln?
*vo kan ikh heer gelt **vek**seln*

How do I get to *(name town)* ...?
Wie komme ich nach...?
*vee **ko**-me ikh nakh...*

### How much is a taxi...?	into town	to the hotel
Wieviel kostet ein Taxi...?	in die Stadt	zum Hotel
*vee**feel** kostet ine taxi...*	*in dee shtat...*	*tsoom ho**tel***

Is there an airport bus to the city centre?
Gibt es einen Airport Bus zum Stadtzentrum?
*gipt es ine-en airport boos tsoom **shtat**-tsentroom*

■ BUS ■ LUGGAGE ■ METRO ■ TAXI

FLUGHAFEN	AIRPORT
ABFLUG	DEPARTURES
BORDKARTE	BOARDING CARD
FLUGSTEIG / GATE	BOARDING GATE

Where do I check in for the flight to...?
Wo ist der Abfertigungsschalter für den Flug nach...?
*voh ist der **ap**-ferti-goongs-shalter foor den flook nakh...*

Which is the departure gate for the flight to...?
Welches Gate hat der Flug nach...?
***vel**-khes gate hat der flook nakh...*

■ YOU MAY HEAR

Sie steigen von Gate Nummer ... ein
*zee **shty**-gen fon gate noomer ... ine*
Boarding will take place at gate number...

Gehen Sie sofort zu Gate Nummer...
***gay**en zee zo-**fort** tsoo gate noomer...*
Go immediately to gate number...

Ihr Flug hat Verspätung
*eer flook hat fer-**shpay**-toong*
Your flight is delayed

■ IF YOU NEED TO CHANGE OR CHECK ON YOUR FLIGHT

I want to change my booking / to cancel my booking
Ich möchte umbuchen / meine Buchung stornieren
*ikh mur'kh-te **oom**-bookhen / mine-e **boo**-khoong shtor-**nee**ren*

I'd like to reconfirm my flight to...
Ich möchte meinen Flug nach ... bestätigen
*ikh mur'kh-te mine-en flook nakh ... be-**shtay**-tigen*

When is the latest I can check in?
Bis wann muß ich spätestens einchecken?
*bis van moos ikh **shpay**-testens **ine**-checken*

Except for ä, ö, ü and ß (which corresponds to double s), the German alphabet is the same as the English. Below are the words used for clarification when spelling something out.

How do you spell it?
Wie schreibt man das?
vee shrybt man das

A as in Anton, b as in Berta
A wie Anton, B wie Berta
ah vee anton bay vee berta

A (ä)	ah (ah **oom**-lowt)	Anton	**an**ton
B	bay	Berta	**ber**ta
C	tsay	Caesar	**tsay**-zar
D	day	Dora	**do**-rah
E	ay	Emil	**ay**-meel
F	ef	Friedrich	**freed**-rikh
G	gay	Gustav	**goos**-tahf
H	hah	Heinrich	**hine**-rikh
I	ee	Ida	**ee**dah
J	yot	Julius	**yoo**-lee-oos
K	kah	Konrad	**kon**rat
L	el	Ludwig	**lood**-vikh
M	em	Martin	**mar**tin
N	en	Nordpol	**nort**-pol
O (ö)	oh (oh **oom**-lowt)	Otto	**o**-toh
P	pay	Paula	**pow**-la
Q	koo	Quelle	**kve**-le
R	ayr	Richard	**rikh**-art
S	es	Siegfried	**zeek**freet
ß	es-**tset**	Eszett	
T	tay	Theodor	**tay**-o-dor
U (ü)	oo (oo **oom**-lowt)	Ulrich	**ool**-rikh
V	fow	Victor	**vik**tor
W	vay	Wilhelm	**vil**helm
X	iks	Xanten	**ksan**-ten
Y	**oop**si-lon		
Z	tset	Zeppelin	**tse**-peleen

12

Yes	**No**	**OK!**
Ya	Nein	Ok!
ya	*nine*	*okay*

Please

Bitte

bi-te

Thank you

Danke

dang-ke

Don't mention it

Bitte

bi-te

Thanks very much

Vielen Dank

feelen dangk

Sir / Mr	**Madam / Mrs / Ms**	**Miss** (*rarely used nowadays*)
Herr	Frau	Fräulein
hayr	*frow*	*froyline*

Excuse me! (to catch attention)

Entschuldigung

entshool-digoong

Excuse me (sorry)

Entschuldigung

entshool-digoong

Pardon?

Wie bitte?

vee bi-te

I don't know

Ich weiß nicht

ikh vice nikht

I don't understand

Ich verstehe nicht

ikh fer-shtay-e nikht

Do you understand?

Verstehen Sie?

fer-shtay-en zee

Do you speak English?

Sprechen Sie Englisch?

shpre-khen zee eng-lish

I speak very little German

Ich spreche sehr wenig Deutsch

ikh shpre-khe zayr vay-nikh doytch

Could you repeat that, please?

Könnten Sie das bitte wiederholen?

kur'n-ten zee das bi-te veeder-hohlen

What is this called in German?

Wie heißt das auf Deutsch?

vee hyst das owf doytch

13

When is the next boat / the next ferry to...?
Wann geht das nächste Schiff / die nächste Fähre nach...?
*van gayt das **nek**-ste shif / dee **nek**-ste **fay**-re nakh...*

Is there a timetable?
Gibt es einen Fahrplan?
*gipt es ine-en **far**plan*

Is there a car ferry to...?
Gibt es eine Autofähre nach...?
*gipt es ine-e **owto**-fay-re nakh...*

How much is...?
Was kostet...?
vas kostet...

a single
die einfache Fahrt
*dee **ine**-fakh-e fart*

return
eine Rückfahrkarte
*ine-e **rook**far-kar-te*

a tourist ticket
eine Touristenkarte
*ine-e too**ris**-ten-kar-te*

a family card
eine Familienkarte
*ine-e fa-**mee**-lee-en-kar-te*

How much is it for a car and ... people?
Was kostet es für ein Auto mit ... Personen?
*vas kostet es foor ine **owto** mit ... per-**zoh**nen?*

How long does the trip take?
Wie lange dauert die Fahrt?
*vee lang-e **dow**-ert dee fart*

When do we get to...?
Wann kommen wir nach...?
van kommen veer nakh...

Where does the boat leave from?
Wo fährt das Schiff ab?
voh fayrt das shif ap

When is the first / the last boat?
Wann geht das erste / das letzte Boot?
*van gayt das **er**-ste / das **let**-ste boht*

Is there somewhere to eat on the boat?
Kann man auf dem Schiff etwas zu essen bekommen?
*kan man owf dem shif **et**vas tsoo essen be-**ko**-men*

■ YOU MAY HEAR

Wollen Sie heute noch zurück?
*vollen zee **hoy**-te nokh tsoo**rook***
Do you want to come back today?

14

My ... hurts	Mein (with der and das) ... tut weh
	Meine (with die) ... tut weh
My ... hurt	Meine (with all plurals) ... tun weh

ankle	der Knöchel	**knur'**-khel
arm	der Arm	arm
back	der Rücken	rooken
bone	der Knochen	**knokh**-en
chin	das Kinn	kin
ear	das Ohr	ohr
elbow	der Ellbogen	**el**-bohgen
eye	das Auge	**ow**-ge
finger	der Finger	**fing**-er
foot	der Fuß	foos
hand	die Hand	hant
head	der Kopf	kopf
heart	das Herz	hayrts
hip	die Hüfte	**hoof**-te
joint	das Gelenk	ge**lenk**
kidney	die Niere	**nee**-re
knee	das Knie	k-nee
leg	das Bein	bine
liver	die Leber	layber
mouth	der Mund	moont
nail	der Nagel	nahgel
neck	der Hals	hals
nose	die Nase	**nah**-ze
stomach	der Magen	**mah**gen
throat	die Kehle	**kay**-le
thumb	der Daumen	dowmen
toe	die Zehe	tsay-e
wrist	das Handgelenk	**hant**-gelenk

■ DOCTOR ■ PHARMACY

15

Can you help me?
Können Sie mir helfen?
kur'-nen zee meer helfen

The car won't start
Der Wagen springt nicht an
der vahgen shpringt nikht an

I've run out of petrol
Ich habe kein Benzin mehr
ikh hah-be kine bentseen mayr

The engine is overheating
Der Motor wird zu heiß
der mohtor veert tsoo hice

I have a flat tyre
Ich habe einen Platten
ikh hah-be ine-en pla-ten

I need water
Ich brauche Wasser
ikh brow-khe vasser

My car has broken down
Ich habe eine Autopanne
ikh hah-be ine-e owto-pan-ne

Can you give me a push?
Können Sie mich anschieben?
kur'-nen zee mikh an-sheeben

Is there a garage near here?
Ist eine Werkstatt in der Nähe?
ist ine-e verk-shtat in der nay-e

The battery is flat
Meine Batterie ist leer
mine-e ba-teree ist layr

I can't get the wheel off
Ich bekomme das Rad nicht ab
ikh be-ko-me das rat nikht ap

The petrol tank / radiator is leaking
Der Tank / Kühler ist leck
der tank / kooler ist leck

Can you tow me to the nearest garage?
Könnten Sie mich bis zur nächsten Werkstatt abschleppen?
kur'n-ten zee mikh bis tsoor nek-sten verk-shtat ap-shleppen

Do you have parts for a (make of car)**...?**
Haben Sie Ersatzteile für einen...?
hah-ben zee erzats-tile-e foor ine-en...

Something is wrong with (see CAR – PARTS)**...**
Es stimmt etwas nicht mit...
es shtimt etvas nikht mit...

Can you put in a new windscreen?
Können Sie eine neue Windschutzscheibe einsetzen?
kur'-nen zee ine-e noy-e vintshoots-shy-be ine-zetsen

■CAR–PARTS

*If you are planning to use public transport, you can buy a multiple ticket card – **eine Streifenkarte**. You have to stamp it either on board the bus/tram/underground or at the bus stop. Other options are **eine Touristenkarte** or **eine Familienkarte**.*

Is there a bus to…?
Gibt es einen Bus nach *(plus place name)* …?
gipt es ine-en boos nakh…

Bonn / Potsdam
Bonn / Potsdam
bon / potsdam

Where does the bus to … leave from?
Wo fährt der Bus zum/zur *(for building, institution)* … ab?
voh fayrt der boos tsoom/tsoor … ab

to the centre
zum Stadtzentrum *(m)*
*tsoom **shtat**-tsentroom*

to the museum
zum Museum *(nt)*
*zum moo-**zay**-oom*

to the art gallery
zur Kunsthalle *(f)*
*tsoor **koonst**-hal-le*

Where can I buy tickets?
Wo kann ich Fahrscheine kaufen?
*voh kann ikh **fahr**-shine-e kowfen*

On the bus?
Im Bus?
im bus

How much is it to…?
Was kostet es bis zum/zur/nach…?
vas kostet es bis tsoom/tsoor/nakh…?

How often are the buses to…?
Wie oft fahren die Busse zum/zur/nach…?
*vee oft **fah**-ren dee **boo**-se tsoom/tsoor/nakh…*

When is the first / the last bus to…?
Wann fährt der erste / der letzte Bus zum/zur/nach…?
*van fayrt der **er**-ste / der **let**-ste boos tsoom/tsoor/nakh…*

Please tell me when to get off
Sagen Sie mir bitte, wann ich aussteigen muß
*zagen see meer **bi**-te van ikh **ows**-shtygen moos*

Please let me off
Kann ich bitte aussteigen
*kan ikh **bi**-te **ows**-shtygen*

This is my stop
Das ist meine Haltestelle
*das ist mine-e **hal**-te-shte-le*

■ METRO ■ TAXI

17

BOARD MEETING	DIE AUFSICHTSRATSITZUNG
CONFERENCE ROOM	DAS KONFERENZZIMMER
MEETING	DIE BESPRECHUNG
MINUTES	DAS PROTOKOLL
SAMPLE	DAS MUSTER
TRADE FAIR	DIE HANDELSMESSE

I'd like to arrange a meeting with...
Ich möchte eine Besprechung mit ... ausmachen
*ikh mur'kh-te ine-e be-**shpre**-khoong mit ... **ows**-makhen*

Are you free to meet...?
Haben Sie Zeit für eine Besprechung...?
***hah**-ben zee tsite foor ine-e be-**shpre**-khoong...*

on April 4th at 11 o'clock
am vierten April um elf Uhr
*am **feer**-ten **april** oom elf oor*

for lunch
bei einem Mittagessen
*by ine-em **mi**tak-essen*

I will send a fax to confirm
Ich schicke ein Fax zur Bestätigung
*ikh shi-ke ine fax tsoor be-**shtay**-tigoong*

I'm staying at Hotel...
Ich wohne im Hotel...
*ikh **voh**-ne im **ho**tel...*

How do I get to your office?
Wie komme ich in Ihr Büro?
*vee **ko**-me ikh in eer boo**roh***

Please let ... know that I will be ... minutes late
Bitte sagen Sie ..., daß ich ... Minuten später komme
***bi**-te zagen zee ... das ikh ... mi**noo**-ten **shpay**ter **ko**-me*

I have an appointment with Herr/Frau...
Ich habe einen Termin mit Herrn/Frau...
*ikh **hah**-be ine-en ter-**meen** mit haym/frow...*

at ... o'clock
um ... Uhr
oom ... oor

I'm ...
Ich bin...
ikh bin...

Here is my card
Hier ist meine Karte
heer ist mine-e kar-te

I'm delighted to meet you at last
Schön, daß wir uns endlich persönlich kennenlernen
*shur'n das veer oons **ent**-likh per-**sur'n**-likh **ken**nen-layr-nen*

My German isn't very good
Mein Deutsch ist nicht sehr gut
mine doytch ist nikht sayr goot

Please speak slowly
Bitte sprechen Sie langsam
***bi**-te **shpre**-khen zee **lang**-zahm*

I'm sorry I'm late
Entschuldigen Sie, daß ich zu spät komme
*ent**shool**-digen zee das ikh tsoo shpayt **ko**-me*

My flight was delayed
Mein Flug hatte Verspätung
*mine flook **hat**-te fer-**shpay**-toong*

May I introduce you to...
Darf ich Ihnen ... vorstellen
*darf ikh ee-nen ... **for**-shtellen*

Can I offer you dinner?
Darf ich Sie zum Essen einladen?
*darf ikh zee tsoom essen **ine**-lahden*

■ YOU MAY HEAR

Haben Sie einen Termin?
hah**-ben zee ine-en ter-**meen
Do you have an appointment?

...ist im Augenblick nicht im Büro
*...ist im **ow**-genblik nikht im boo**roh***
... isn't in the office at the moment

Er/Sie kommt in ein paar Minuten wieder
*er/zee komt in ein pahr mi**noo**-ten **vee**der*
He/She will be back in a few minutes

■ FAX ■ LETTERS ■ OFFICE ■ TELEPHONE

Local tourist offices should have details of campsites and prices.

Do you have a list of campsites with prices?
Haben Sie eine Liste von Campingplätzen mit Preisen?
*hah-ben zee ine-e **lis**-te fon **kam**ping-pletsen mit **pry**-zen*

Is the campsite sheltered?
Liegt der Campingplatz geschützt?
*leekt der **kam**ping-platz ge-**shootst***

How far is the lake?
Wie weit ist es bis zum See?
vee vite ist es bis tsoom zay

Is there a restaurant?
Gibt es ein Restaurant?
*gipt es ine restoh-**rong***

Is there a shop?
Gibt es einen Laden?
*gipt es ine-en **lah**-den*

Do you have any vacancies?
Haben Sie noch Plätze frei?
*hah-ben zee nokh **plet**-se fry*

Are showers...	**Is hot water...**	**Is electricity...**
Ist Duschen...	Ist Heißwasser...	Ist Strom...
ist doo-shen...	*ist **hice**-wasser...*	*ist shtrohm...*

...included in the price?
...im Preis inbegriffen?
...im price in-be-griffen

We'd like to stay for ... nights
Wir möchten ... Nächte bleiben
*veer mur'kh-ten ... **nekh**-te **bly**-ben*

How much is it per night...?
Was kostet die Nacht...?
vas kostet dee nakht...

for a tent
pro Zelt
pro tselt

per person
pro Person
*pro per-**zohn***

Can we camp here overnight? *(for tent)*
Können wir über Nacht hier zelten?
*kur'-nen veer oober nakht heer **tsel**-ten*

■ **SIGHTSEEING & TOURIST OFFICE**

*If you park in a **Blaue Zone** you will need a parking disk or ticket.*

ALLE RICHTUNGEN	ALL ROUTES
AUSFAHRT	EXIT
AUTOBAHN	MOTORWAY
EINBAHNSTRASSE	ONE-WAY STREET
EINORDNEN	GET IN LANE
GEFAHR	DANGER
GESPERRT	ROAD CLOSED
GESCHWINDIGKEITSBESCHRÄNKUNG	SPEED LIMIT
HALT	STOP
LANGSAM FAHREN	SLOW DOWN
PARKEN VERBOTEN	NO PARKING
STADTZENTRUM	TOWN CENTRE
VORFAHRT ACHTEN	GIVE WAY

Can I/we park here?
Kann man hier parken?
*kan man heer **par**ken*

Do I/we need a parking disk?
Braucht man eine Parkscheibe?
*browkht man ine-e **park**-shy-be*

How long can I/we park for?
Wie lange darf man hier parken?
*vee lang-e darf man heer **par**ken*

We're going to....
Wir fahren nach...
veer fah-ren nakh...

What's the best route?
Was ist der beste Weg?
*vas ist der **bes**-te vayk*

Will there be a lot of traffic on the motorway?
Ist viel Betrieb auf der Autobahn?
*ist feel be-**treep** owf der **ow**to-bahn*

Is the pass open?
Ist der Paß offen?
*ist der pas **of**fen*

Do I/we need snow chains?
Braucht man Schneeketten?
*browkht man **shnay**-ketten*

■ BREAKDOWNS ■ PETROL STATION

21

| DRIVING LICENCE | DER FÜHRERSCHEIN |
| REVERSE GEAR | DER RÜCKWÄRTSGANG |

I want to hire a car
Ich möchte ein Auto mieten
*ickh mur'kh-te ine **ow**to meeten*

for one day
für einen Tag
foor ine-en tahk

for ... days
für ... Tage
foor ... ta-ge

How much is the car...?
Was kostet der Wagen...?
vas kostet der vahgen...

per day
pro Tag
proh tahk

per week
pro Woche
proh vo-khe

How much is the deposit?
Wie hoch ist die Kaution?
*vee hokh ist dee kow-**tsyon***

Is there a mileage (kilometre) charge?
Verlangen Sie eine Kilometergebühr?
*fer-**lang**en zee ine-e keelo-**may**ter-geboor*

How much is it?
Wieviel ist das?
*vee**feel** ist das*

Does the price include fully comprehensive insurance?
Ist im Preis eine Vollkaskoversicherung inbegriffen?
*ist im price ine-e **fol**-kasko-fer-**zikh**eroong **in**-be-griffen*

Must I return the car here?
Muß ich das Auto hierher zurückbringen?
*moos ikh das **ow**to **heer**-her tsoo**rook**-bringen*

By what time?
Bis wann?
bis van

I'd like to leave it in...
Ich würde es gerne in ... abgeben
*ikh voor-de es gern-e in ... **ap**-gayben*

Please show me how the controls work
Bitte erklären Sie mir die Schalter
*bi-te er-**klay**-ren zee meer dee **shal**-ter*

■ **YOU MAY HEAR**

Bitte bringen Sie das Auto vollgetankt zurück
*bi-te bringen zee das **ow**to **fol**-ge-tankt tsoo**rook***
Please return the car with a full tank

The ... doesn't work	The ... don't work
Der/Die/Das ... funktioniert nicht	Die ... funktionieren nicht
*der/dee/das...foonk-tsyoh-**neert** nikht*	*dee...foonk-tsyoh-**nee**ren nikht*

accelerator	das Gaspedal	**gas**-paydal
battery	die Batterie	ba-te**ree**
bonnet	die Motorhaube	**moh**tor-how-be
brakes	die Bremsen	bremzen
central locking	die Zentralverriegelung	tsen**tral**-fer-ree-geloong
choke	der Choke	choke
clutch	die Kupplung	**koop**loong
distributor	der Verteiler	fayr-**tyler**
engine	der Motor	moh**tor**
exhaust pipe	das Auspuffrohr	**ows**poof-rohr
fanbelt	der Keilriemen	**kile**-reemen
fuse	die Sicherung	**zikh**-eroong
gears	das Getriebe	ge**tree**-be
handbrake	die Handbremse	**hant**brem-ze
headlights	die Scheinwerfer	**shine**-verfer
ignition	die Zündung	**tsoon**-doong
indicator	der Blinker	blinker
points	die Unterbrecher-kontakte	oonter-**brekh**-er-kon**tak**-te
radiator	der Kühler	kooler
rear lights	das Rücklicht	**rook**-likht
seat belt	der Sicherheitsgurt	**zikh**er-hites-goort
spare wheel	der Ersatzreifen	er**zats**-ry-fen
spark plugs	die Zündkerzen	**tsoont**-kayrtsen
steering	die Lenkung	**len**koong
tyre	der Reifen	**ry**-fen
wheel	das Rad	rat
windscreen	die Windschutzscheibe	**vint**shoots-shy-be
-- wiper	der Scheibenwischer	**shy**ben-visher

■ BREAKDOWNS ■ PETROL STATION

23

I'd like to wish you...
Ich wünsche Ihnen...
*ikh **voon**-she ee-nen...*

I'd like to wish you... *(familiar)*
Ich wünsche dir...
*ikh **voon**-she deer...*

Merry Christmas!
Frohe Weihnachten!
*froh-e **vy**-nakhten*

Happy New Year!
ein Frohes Neues Jahr!
*ine **froh**-es **noy**-es yahr*

Happy Easter!
Frohe Ostern!
*froh-e **oh**-stern*

Happy (Saint's) Name Day!
Alles Gute zum Namenstag!
*a-les **goo**-te tsoom **nah**-mens-tahk*

Happy birthday!
Herzlichen Glückwunsch zum Geburtstag!
*hayrts-lihken **glook**-voonsh tsoom ge-**boorts**-tahk*

Have a good trip!
Gute Reise!
***goo**-te **ry**-ze*

Best wishes!
Viele Grüße!
*fee-le **groo**-se*

Welcome!
Herzlich willkommen!
*hayrts-lihk **vil**-kommen*

Enjoy your meal!
Guten Appetit!
goo**-ten apay-**teet

Thanks, and the same to you!
Danke, gleichfalls!
***dang**-ke **glykh**-fals*

Cheers!
Prost! or Prosit!
*prohst / **proh**-zit*

To your health!
Zum Wohl!
tsoom vohl

Congratulations! *(having a baby, getting married, etc.)*
Herzliche Glückwünsche!
*hayrts-lihk-e **glook**-voon-she*

■ LETTERS ■ MAKING FRIENDS

AB 12 JAHREN/AB 14 JAHREN	**SUITABLE FOR CHILDREN OVER 12/14**
OmU	**ORIGINAL VERSION WITH SUBTITLES**
VORSTELLUNG	**PERFORMANCE**

What's on at the cinema?
Was gibt es im Kino?
vas gipt es im keeno

When does the film start?
Wann fängt der Film an?
van fengt der film an

Is the film dubbed?
Ist der Film synchronisiert?
*ist der film zoon-kroh-ni***zeert**

How much is it to get in?
Was kostet der Eintritt?
*vas kostet der **ine**-trit*

Two for (name film) ...
Zwei für...
tsvy foor...

What films have you seen recently?
Welche Filme haben Sie in der letzten Zeit gesehen?
***vel**-khe film-e **hah**-ben zee in der **lets**-ten tsite ge**zay**-en*

What is (English name of film) called in German?
Wie heißt ... auf Deutsch?
vee hyst ... owf doytch

Who is your favourite actress?
Wer ist Ihre Lieblingsschauspielerin?
*vayr ist ee-re **leep**lings-show-shpeelerin*

Who is your favourite actor?
Wer ist Ihr Lieblingsschauspieler?
*vayr ist eer **leep**lings-show-shpeeler*

■ YOU MAY HEAR

Für Kino 1/2...	**ist ausverkauft**
foor keeno ines/tsvy...	*ist **ows**-ferkowft*
For screen 1/2...	**it's sold out**

■ ENTERTAINMENT ■ LEISURE/INTERESTS

women

sizes	
UK	EC
10	36
12	38
14	40
16	42
18	44
20	46

men - suits

sizes	
UK	EC
36	46
38	48
40	50
42	52
44	54
46	56

shoes

sizes			
UK	EC	UK	EC
2	35	8	42
3	36	9	43
4	37	10	44
5	38	11	45
6	39		
7	41		

May I try this on?
Kann ich das anprobieren?
*kan ikh das **an**proh-beeren*

Where are the changing rooms?
Wo sind die Umkleidekabinen?
*voh zint dee **oom**-kly-de-ka-**bee**nen*

Do you have this a size...?
Haben Sie das eine Größe...?
***hah**-ben zee das ine-e grur'-se...*

bigger	**smaller**
größer	kleiner
grur'-ser	*kline-er*

Do you have this in other colours?
Haben Sie das noch in anderen Farben?
***hah**-ben zee das nokh in **an**-de-ren farben*

It's too big
Es ist zu groß
es ist tsoo grohs

It's too small
Es ist zu klein
es ist tsoo kline

It's too expensive
Es ist zu teuer
*es ist tsoo **toy**-er*

I'm just looking
Ich schaue mich nur um
ikh show-e mikh noor oom

I'll take it
Ich nehme es
*ikh **nay**-me es*

■ YOU MAY HEAR

Welche Größe haben Sie?
***vel**-khe grur'-se **hah**-ben zee*
What size are you?

Paßt es?
past es
Does it fit you?

■ NUMBERS ■ PAYING ■ SHOPPING

COTTON	DIE BAUMWOLLE	SILK	DIE SEIDE
LACE	DIE SPITZE	SUEDE	DAS WILDLEDER
LEATHER	DAS LEDER	WOOL	DIE WOLLE

belt	der Gürtel	**goor**-tel
blouse	die Bluse	**bloo**-se
bra	der Büstenhalter	**boos**-ten-halter
coat	der Mantel	**man**tel
dress	das Kleid	klite
gloves	die Handschuhe	**hant**-shoo-e
hat	der Hut	hoot
jacket	das Jackett	ya**ket**
knickers	der Slip	slip
nightdress	das Nachthemd	**nakht**-hemt
pyjamas	der Pyjama	poo-**jah**-ma
raincoat	der Regenmantel	**ray**gen-mantel
sandals	die Sandalen	zan-**dah**-len
scarf (silk)	das Kopftuch	**kopf**-tookh
scarf (wool)	das Halstuch	**hals**-tookh
shirt	das Hemd	hemt
shorts	die Shorts	shorts
skirt	der Rock	rock
slippers	die Pantoffeln	pan**tof**-feln
socks	die Socken	zocken
suit (man's)	der Anzug	**an**-tsook
suit (woman's)	das Kostüm	kos-**toom**
swimsuit	der Badeanzug	**bah**-de-antsook
tie	die Krawatte	krava-te
tights	die Strumpfhose	**shtroompf**-hoh-ze
tracksuit	der Trainingsanzug	**train**ings-antsook
trousers	die Hose	**hoh**-ze
underpants	der Slip	slip
zip	der Reißverschluß	**rice**-fer-shloos

> Two key words for describing colours in German are:
> **hell**   light   **dunkel**   dark

black	schwarz	shvarts
blue	blau	blow
navy blue	marineblau	ma**ree**-ne-blow
brown	braun	brown
cream	creme	**kray**-me
crimson	purpurrot	**poor**poor-roht
gold	gold	golt
green	grün	groon
grey	grau	grow
lemon	zitronengelb	tsi-**troh**nen-gelp
orange	orange	o**ron**-je
pink	rosa	**roh**za
purple	violett	vee-o-**let**
red	rot	roht
silver	silber	zilber
turquoise	türkis	toor**kis**
white	weiß	vice
yellow	gelb	gelp

■ SHAPE

big	groß	grohs
fat	dick	dik
flat	flach	flakh
long	lang	lang
narrow	eng	eng
round	rund	roont
small	klein	kline
square	quadratisch	kva-**drah**tish
tall	groß	grohs
thick	dick	dik
thin	dünn	doon
tiny	winzig	**vin**zig
wide	weit	vite

The ... doesn't work
Der/Die/Das ... funktioniert nicht
*der/dee/das...foonk-tsyoh-**neert** nikht*

The ... don't work
Die ... funktionieren nicht
*die...foonk-tsyoh-**nee**ren nikht*

light	**lock**	**toilet**	**heating**
das Licht	das Schloß	die Toilette	die Heizung
das likht	*das shlos*	*dee twa-**le**-te*	*dee **hyt**-soong*

There's a problem with the room
Ich habe ein Problem mit dem Zimmer
*ikh **hah**-be ine proh-**blaym** mit dem **tsi**mmer*

It's too noisy
Es ist zu laut
es ist tsoo lowt

It's too hot / too cold
Es ist zu warm / zu kalt
es ist tsoo varm / tsoo kalt

It's too small
Es ist zu klein
es ist tsoo kline

It's too hot / too cold (food)
Das ist zu heiß / zu kalt
das ist tsoo hice / tsoo kalt

This isn't what I ordered
Das habe ich nicht bestellt
*das **hah**-be ikh nikht be**shtelt***

To whom can I complain?
Bei wem kann ich mich beschweren?
*by vaym kan ikh mikh be-**shvay**ren*

I want my money back
Ich möchte mein Geld zurück
*ikh mur'kh-te mine gelt tsoo**rook***

The goods were damaged in transit
Die Waren wurden beim Transport beschädigt
*dee **vah**ren **voor**-den bime trans**port** be-**shay**dikt*

We have been waiting for a very long time
Wir warten schon sehr lange
*veer **var**-ten shohn sayr lang-e*

The bill is not correct
Die Rechnung stimmt nicht
*dee **rekh**-noong shtimt nikht*

■ PROBLEMS ■ REPAIRS ■ ROOM SERVICE

COMPUTER	DER COMPUTER
DATABASE	DIE DATENBANK
FILE	DIE DATEI
FLOPPY DISK	DIE DISKETTE
FONT	DIE SCHRIFTART
HARD DISK	DIE FESTPLATTE
LASER PROOFS	DER AUSDRUCK VOM LASERDRUCKER
MOUSE	DIE MAUS
PRINTER	DER DRUCKER
SCREEN	DER BILDSCHIRM

What computer do you use?
Was für einen Computer benutzen Sie?
*vas foor ine-en kom**pu**ter be**noot**sen zee*

Is it IBM compatible?
Ist er IBM-kompatibel?
*ist er ee-bay-em kom-pah-**tee**bel*

Do you have E-mail?
Haben Sie eine elektronische Mailbox?
*hah-ben zee ine-e elek-**troh**-nish-e **mail**box*

What's the address?
Wie ist die Adresse?
*vee ist dee a-**dre**-se*

Do you have a database?
Haben Sie eine Datenbank?
*hah-ben zee ine-e **da**ten-bank*

How often is it updated?
Wie oft wird sie aktualisiert?
*vee oft virt zee aktoo-ah-li**zeert***

Please send it on a floppy disk
Bitte schicken Sie es uns auf Diskette
*bi-te shicken zee es oons owf dis-**ke**-te*

What word processing package do you use?
Welches Textsystem benutzen Sie?
*vel-khes **text**-soostaym be**noot**sen zee*

Can I have an ASCII file?
Kann ich eine ASCII-Datei haben?
*kan ikh ine-e **ah**-skee-dah-ty **hah**-ben*

■ **OFFICE**

*With the Single European Market, travellers are subject only to highly selective spot checks. The red and green channels no longer apply within the EC. There is no restriction, either by quantity or value, on goods purchased by travellers in another EC country provided they are **for their own personal use** (guidelines have been published). If you are unsure of certain items, check with the customs officials as to whether payment of duty is required.*

AUSWEISKONTROLLE / PASSKONTROLLE	PASSPORT CONTROL
EG	EC
PERSONALAUSWEIS	IDENTITY DOCUMENT
ZOLL	CUSTOMS

Do I have to pay duty on this?
Muß ich das verzollen?
*moos ikh das fer-**tso**llen*

I bought this in ... as a gift
Ich habe das in ... als Geschenk gekauft
*ikh **hah**-be das in ... als ge-**shenk** ge**kowft***

It is for my own personal use
Es ist für meinen persönlichen Gebrauch
*es ist foor mine-en per-**zur'n**-likhen ge-**browkh***

We are on our way to... *(if in transit to another country)*
Wir sind auf der Durchreise nach...
*veer zint owf der **doorkh**-ry-ze nakh...*

The children are on this passport
Die Kinder stehen auch in diesem Paß
*dee **kin**der **shtay**-en owkh in dee-zem pass*

I have a visa
Ich habe ein Visum
*ikh **hah**-be ine **vee**zoom*

days

MONDAY	MONTAG
TUESDAY	DIENSTAG
WEDNESDAY	MITTWOCH
THURSDAY	DONNERSTAG
FRIDAY	FREITAG
SATURDAY	SAMSTAG
SUNDAY	SONNTAG

months

JANUARY	JANUAR
FEBRUARY	FEBRUAR
MARCH	MÄRZ
APRIL	APRIL
MAY	MAI
JUNE	JUNI
JULY	JULI
AUGUST	AUGUST
SEPTEMBER	SEPTEMBER
OCTOBER	OKTOBER
NOVEMBER	NOVEMBER
DECEMBER	DEZEMBER

seasons

SPRING	DER FRÜHLING
SUMMER	DER SOMMER
AUTUMN	DER HERBST
WINTER	DER WINTER

What is today's date?
Was für ein Datum haben wir heute?
*was foor ine **dah**toom **hah**-ben veer **hoy**-te*

It's the 5th of March 1993
Heute ist der fünfte März neunzehnhundertdreiundneunzig
***hoy**-te ist der **foonf**-te merts **noyn**tsayn-hoondert-dry-oont-**noyn**-tsikh*

on Saturday	**on Saturdays**	**every Saturday**
am Samstag	samstags	jeden Samstag
*am **zams**tah*	*__zams__tahks*	*__yay__-den **zams**tah*

this Saturday	**next Saturday**	**last Saturday**
diesen Samstag	nächsten Samstag	letzten Samstag
***dee**zen **zams**tah*	***nekh**-sten **zams**tah*	***lets**-ten **zams**tah*

in June	**at the beginning of June**	**at the end of June**
im Juni	Anfang Juni	Ende Juni
*im **yoo**nee*	***an**fang **yoo**nee*	*en-de **yoo**nee*

before summer	**during the summer**	**after summer**
vor dem Sommer	im Sommer	nach dem Sommer
*for dem **zom**mer*	*im **zom**mer*	*nakh dem **zom**mer*

■ NUMBERS

FILLING	DIE PLOMBE
CROWN	DIE KRONE
DENTURES	DAS GEBISS
A TEMPORARY REPAIR	EINE PROVISORISCHE REPARATUR

I need a dentist
Ich brauche einen Zahnarzt
*ikh **brow**-khe in-en **tsahn**artst*

He / She has toothache
Er / Sie hat Zahnschmerzen
*er / zee hat **tsahn**-shmer-tsen*

Can you do a temporary filling?
Können Sie mir eine provisorische Plombe machen?
*kur'-nen zee meer ine-e provi-**zor**ish-e **plom**-be makhen*

I think I have an abscess
Ich glaube, ich habe einen Abszess
*ikh **glow**-be ikh **hah**-be ine-en apst**sess***

It hurts
Das tut weh
das toot vay

Can you give me something for the pain?
Können Sie mir etwas gegen die Schmerzen geben?
*kur'-nen zee meer **et**vas **gay**-gen dee **shmer**-tsen **gay**ben*

Can you repair my dentures?
Können Sie mein Gebiß reparieren?
*kur'-nen zee mine ge**biss** raypa-**ree**ren*

Do I have to pay now?
Muß ich das gleich bezahlen?
*moos ikh das **glykh** be**tsah**-len*

How much will it be?
Wie teuer wird es?
*vee **toy**-er virt es*

I need a receipt for my insurance
Ich brauche eine Quittung für meine Krankenkasse
*ikh **brow**-khe ine-e **kvi**-toong foor mine-e **krang**-ken-ka-se*

■ **YOU MAY HEAR**

Bitte weit aufmachen
*bi-te vite **owf**-makhen*
Please open wide

Möchten Sie eine Schmerzspritze?
*mur'kh-ten zee ine-e **shmerts**-shprit-se*
Do you want an injection?

OPPOSITE	GEGENÜBER	*gaygen-oober*
NEXT TO	NEBEN	*nayben*
NEAR TO	IN DER NÄHE VON	*in der nay-e fon*
TRAFFIC LIGHTS	DIE AMPEL	*dee ampel*
AT THE CORNER	AN DER ECKE	*an der e-ke*

Excuse me!
Entschuldigung!
entshool-digoong

How do I get to...?
Wie komme ich zum/zur/nach...?
vee ko-me ikh tsoom/tsoor/nakh...

to the station
zum Bahnhof *(m)*
tsoom bahn-hohf

to the castle
zur Burg *(f)*
tsoor boork

to Bonn
nach Bonn
nakh bon

We're looking for...
Wir suchen...
veer zookhen...

Is it far?
Ist es weit?
ist es vite

Can I walk there?
Kann ich dahin laufen?
kan ikh dahin lowfen

We're lost *(on foot)*
Wir haben uns verlaufen
veer hah-ben oons fer-lowfen

We're lost *(in car)*
Wir haben uns verfahren
veer hah-ben oons fer-fahren

Is this the right way to...?
Bin ich hier richtig zum/zur/nach...?
bin ikh heer rikhtikh tsoom/tsoor/nakh...

How do I get onto the motorway?
Wie komme ich zur Autobahn?
vee ko-me ikh tsoor owto-bahn

Can you show me on the map?
Können Sie mir das auf der Karte zeigen?
kur'-nen zee meer das owf der kar-te tsy-gen

■ **YOU MAY HEAR**

Immer geradeaus
immer gayrah-de-ows
Straight on

Biegen Sie links / rechts ab
bee-gen zee links / rekhts ap
Turn left / right

■ **BASICS** ■ **MAPS, GUIDES & NEWSPAPERS**

What facilities do you have for disabled people?
Welche Einrichtungen haben Sie für Behinderte?
*vel-khe **ine**-rikht-toongen **hah**-ben zee foor be-**hin**-der-te*

Do you have toilets for the disabled?
Haben Sie Toiletten für Behinderte?
***hah**-ben zee twa-**le**-ten foor be-**hin**-der-te*

Do you have any bedrooms on the ground floor?
Haben Sie Zimmer im Erdgeschoß?
***hah**-ben zee **tsi**mmer im **ert**-geshos*

Do you have a lift?
Haben Sie einen Aufzug?
***hah**-ben zee ine-en **owf**tsook*

Where is the lift?
Wo ist der Aufzug?
*voh ist der **owf**tsook*

Are there any ramps for wheelchairs?
Haben Sie Rampen für Rollstühle?
***hah**-ben zee **ram**pen foor **rol**-shtoo-le*

How many steps are there?
Wieviele Stufen sind es?
*vee**fee**-le **shtoo**-fen zint es*

How wide are the doors?
Wie breit sind die Türen?
*vee brite zint dee **too**ren*

Where is the wheelchair-accessible entrance?
Wo ist der Eingang für Rollstuhlfahrer?
*voh ist der **ine**-gang foor **rol**-shtool-fahrer*

Is there an induction loop for the hard of hearing?
Haben Sie eine Induktionsschleife für Schwerhörige?
***hah**-ben zee ein-e in-dook-**tsyohns**-shly-fe foor shvayr-**hur'**-ri-ge*

Is there a reduction for the disabled?
Gibt es Ermäßigung für Behinderte?
*gipt es er-**may**-sigoong foor be-**hin**-der-te*

■ ACCOMMODATION ■ HOTEL

KRANKENHAUS	HOSPITAL
AMBULANZ	OUT-PATIENTS
SPRECHSTUNDEN	SURGERY HOURS

I need a doctor
Ich brauche einen Arzt
*ikh **brow**-khe ine-en artst*

My son / My daughter is ill
Mein Sohn / Meine Tochter ist krank
*mine zohn / mine-e **tokh**ter ist krank*

I have a pain here (point)
Ich habe Schmerzen hier
*ikh **hah**-be **shmer**tsen heer*

He / She has a high temperature
Er / Sie hat hohes Fieber
*er / zee hat **hoh**-es **fee**ber*

I'm diabetic
Ich habe Zucker
*ikh **hah**-be tsooker*

I'm pregnant
Ich bin schwanger
*ikh bin **shvang**er*

I'm on the pill
Ich nehme die Pille
*ikh **nay**-me dee **pi**-le*

I'm allergic to penicillin
Ich bin allergisch gegen Penizillin
*ikh bin a-**ler**-gish **gay**-gen peni-tsi**leen***

My blood group is...
Meine Blutgruppe ist...
*mine-e **bloot**groo-pe ist...*

Will he / she have to go to hospital?
Muß er / sie ins Krankenhaus?
*moos er / zee ins **kran**ken-hows*

Will I have to pay?
Muß ich gleich bezahlen?
*moos ikh glykh be**tsah**-len*

How much will it cost?
Was wird es kosten?
vas virt es kosten

I need a receipt for the insurance
Ich brauche eine Quittung für meine Versicherung
*ikh **brow**-khe ine-e **kvi**-toong foor mine-e fer**zikh**-eroong*

■ **YOU MAY HEAR**

Sie müssen ins Krankenhaus
*zee moossen ins **kran**ken-hows*
You will have to go to hospital

Ich muß Sie röntgen
*ikh moos zee **rur'nt**-gen*
I'll have to give you an X-ray

■ BODY ■ EMERGENCIES ■ PHARMACY

36

a black coffee
einen schwarzen Kaffee
*ine-en **shvar**-tsen ka**fay***

a white coffee
einen Kaffee mit Sahne
*ine-en ka**fay** mit **zah**-ne*

...please
...bitte
*...**bi**-te*

a tea...
einen Tee...
ine-en tay...

with milk
mit Frischmilch
*mit **frish**-milkh*

with lemon
mit Zitrone
*mit tsi**troh**-ne*

no sugar
ohne Zucker
***oh**-ne tsooker*

for two
für zwei
foor tsvy

for me
für mich
foor mikh

for him / her
für ihn / sie
foor een / zee

for us
für uns
foor oons

with ice
mit Eis
mit ice

a lager
ein helles Bier
ine he-les beer

a bitter
ein Altbier
ine altbeer

a half pint
ein Kleines
ine kline-es

a pint (approx.)
ein Großes
ine groh-ses

A bottle of mineral water
Eine Flasche Mineralwasser
*ine-e **fla**-she mi-ne**rahl**-vasser*

sparkling
mit Kohlensäure
*mit **kohl**en-zoy-re*

still
still
shtill

Would you like a drink?
Möchten Sie etwas trinken?
*mur'kh-ten zee **et**vas **trin**ken*

What will you have?
Was darf es sein?
vas darf es zine

I'm very thirsty
Ich habe großen Durst
*ikh **hah**-be groh-sen doorst*

I'd like a cool drink
Ich möchte ein kühles Getränk
*ikh mur'kh-te ine **koo**-les ge-**trenk***

Do you have anything non-alcoholic?
Haben Sie auch Getränke ohne Alkohol?
***hah**-ben zee owkh ge-**treng**-ke **oh**-ne **al**-kohol*

■ **OTHER DRINKS TO TRY**

ein Diesel Coca-Cola and lemonade
ein dunkles Bier dark beer similar to brown ale
einen Fruchtsaft fruit juice
eine heiße Schokolade rich-tasting hot chocolate
ein Pils a strong, slightly bitter lager
ein Radler a type of shandy

■ **EATING OUT** ■ **WINES & SPIRITS**

*In Germany the main meal of the day is lunch – **Mittagessen**. Breakfast – **Frühstück** – is also often a substantial meal. Look out for breakfast buffets – **Frühstücksbüffet**. Those preferring vegetarian dishes, turn to the VEGETARIAN topic for further phrases.*

Where can we have a snack?
Wo kann man hier eine Kleinigkeit essen?
*voh kan man heer ine-e **kline**-ikh-kite essen*

Can you recommend a good local restaurant?
Können Sie ein gutes Restaurant am Ort empfehlen?
***kur'**-nen zee ine **goo**-tes restoh-**rong** am ort emp-**fay**len*

I'd like to book a table for ... people
Ich möchte einen Tisch für ... Personen reservieren
*ikh mur'kh-te ine-en tish foor ... per-**zoh**nen ray-zer-**vee**ren*

for tonight...	for tomorrow night...	for 8 pm
für heute abend...	für morgen abend...	für acht Uhr
*foor **hoy**-te **ah**bent...*	*foor **mor**gen **ah**bent...*	*foor akht oor*

The menu, please
Die Speisekarte, bitte
*dee **shpy**-ze-kar-te **bi**-te*

What is the dish of the day?
Was ist das Tagesgericht?
*vas ist das **tah**ges-gerikht*

Have you a set-price menu?
Haben Sie eine Tageskarte?
***hah**-ben zee ine-e **tah**ges-kar-te?*

Can you recommend a local dish?
Können Sie eine Spezialität der Gegend empfehlen?
***kur'**-nen zee ine-e shpe-tsee-ali-**tayt** der **gay**gent emp-**fay**len*

What is in this?	I'll have this
Was ist das?	Ich nehme das
vas ist das	*ikh **nay**-me das*

Excuse me!	more bread...	more water...	please
Entschuldigung	noch Brot...	noch Wasser...	bitte
*ent**shool**-digoong*	*nokh broht...*	*nokh vasser...*	***bi**-te*

The bill, please	Is service included?
Zahlen, bitte	Ist die Bedienung inbegriffen?
*tsah-len **bi**-te*	*ist dee be-**dee**noong **in**-be-griffen*

■ EATING PLACES

Restaurant *restaurant usually also offering set-price meals*

Gaststätte *a cross between a restaurant and pub where the food is washed down with beer*

Weinstube *wine bar where there is often a buffet*

Imbiss-Stube *snack bar serving tasty dishes*

Beisel *bar/bistro serving simple Austrian dishes (Austria)*

Konditorei *cake shop often serving mouth-watering pastries*

■ SUPPEN	SOUPS
Aalsuppe	*eel soup*
Bohnensuppe	*thick bean and bacon soup*
Erbsensuppe	*pea soup*
Fischsuppe	*fish soup*
Gemüsesuppe	*vegetable soup*
Gulaschsuppe	*spicy meat soup with paprika*
Linsensuppe	*lentil soup*
Nudelsuppe	*noodle soup*
Spargelcremesuppe	*cream of asparagus soup*

■ VORSPEISEN	STARTERS/FIRST COURSES
Artischocken	*artichokes*
Gänseleberpastete	*goose liver pâté*
Matjeshering	*salted herring*
Spargel	*asparagus*
Krabbencocktail	*prawn cocktail*

■ FLEISCHGERICHTE	MEAT DISHES
Aufschnitt	*sliced cold meats*
Bratwurst	*fried sausage*
Gulasch	*stewed beef with paprika*
Hammel	*mutton*
Hühnchen	*chicken*
Kalbsbraten	*roast veal*

CONT...

Kalbskoteletts	veal cutlets
Kalbsleber	calf's liver
Klops	rissole
Knackwurst	hot spicy sausage
Lamm	lamb
Leberwurst	liver sausage
Nieren	kidneys
Ragout	stew
Rinderbraten	roast beef
Rindfleisch	beef
Rindsrouladen	beef olives
Schinken	ham
Schnitzel	escalope
Schweinebraten	roast pork
Speck	bacon
Wiener Schnitzel	veal escalope fried in breadcrumbs
Wildbraten	roast venison

■ FISCHGERICHTE

FISH AND SEAFOOD

Aal	eel
Austern	oysters
Barsch	perch
Fischklöße	fish dumplings
Flunder	flounder
Forelle Steiermark	trout fillet with bacon in white sauce
Gegrillter Lachs	grilled salmon
Hecht	pike
Hummer	lobster
Kabeljau	cod
Karpfen in Bier	carp poached in beer with herbs
Languste	lobster
Schellfisch	haddock
Scholle	plaice

Seezunge	sole
Steinbutt	turbot
Thunfisch	tuna fish
Wiener Fischfilets	fish fillets baked in sour cream sauce

■ GEMÜSE & KLÖSSE — VEGETABLES & DUMPLINGS

Artischocken	artichokes
Blumenkohl	cauliflower
Bratkartoffeln	fried potatoes
Dampfnudel	yeast dumplings
Erbsen	peas
Gemüseplatte	mixed vegetables
Kartoffelpüree	mashed potato
Kloß	potato dumpling
Leipziger Allerlei	peas, carrots, cauliflower, cabbage
Nudeln	noodles
Rösti	fried diced potatoes, onions, bacon
Salzkartoffeln	boiled potatoes
Sauerkraut	shredded pickled white cabbage

■ SALAT — SALAD

Bohnensalat	bean salad
Gemischter Salat	mixed salad
Grüner Salat	green salad
Kartoffelsalat	potato salad

■ NACHSPEISEN — DESSERTS

Apfelstrudel	flaky pastry filled with apple, spices
Eis	ice cream
Eisbecher	knickerbocker glory
Frucht	fresh fruit
Obstsalat	fruit salad
Linzertorte	latticed tart with jam topping

■ DRINKS ■ VEGETARIAN ■ WINES & SPIRITS

POLIZEI	POLICE
KRANKENWAGEN / AMBULANZ	AMBULANCE
FEUERWEHR	FIRE BRIGADE
UNFALLSTATION	CASUALTY DEPARTMENT

Help!
Hilfe!
hil-fe

Fire!
Feuer!
foy-er

Can you help me?
Können Sie mir helfen?
kur'n-en zee meer helf-fen

There's been an accident
Ein Unfall ist passiert
ine oonfal ist paseert

Someone is injured
Es ist jemand verletzt worden
es ist yaymant ferletst vorden

Someone has been knocked down by a car
Es ist jemand überfahren worden
es ist yaymant oober-fahren vorden

Please call...
Bitte rufen Sie...
bi-te roofen zee...

the police
die Polizei
dee poli-tsy

an ambulance
einen Krankenwagen
ine-en kranken-vahgen

Where is the police station?
Wo ist die Polizeiwache?
vo ist dee poli-tsy-va-khe

I want to report a theft
Ich möchte einen Diebstahl melden
ikh mur'kh-te ine-en deep-shtahl melden

I've been robbed
Man hat mich beraubt
man hat mikh be-rowpt

I've been attacked
Man hat mich überfallen
man hat mikh oober-fallen

Someone has stolen...
Jemand hat ... gestohlen
yaymant hat ... geshtoh-len

my money
mein Geld
mine gelt

my passport
meinen Paß
mine-en pas

My car has been broken into
Man hat mein Auto aufgebrochen
man hat mine owto owf-gebro-khen

My car has been stolen
Man hat mein Auto gestohlen
*man hat mine **ow**to ge**shtoh**-len*

I've been raped
Ich bin vergewaltigt worden
*ikh bin fer-ge**val**-tikht **vor**den*

I want to speak to a policewoman
Ich möchte mit einer Polizistin sprechen
*ikh mur'kh-te mit ine-er poli-**tsis**-tin **shpre**-khen*

I need to make an urgent telephone call
Ich muß dringend telefonieren
*ikh moos **drin**gent taylay-fo-**nee**ren*

I need a report for my insurance
Ich brauche einen Bericht für meine Versicherung
*ikh **brow**-khe ine-en be**rikht** foor mine-e fer**zhikh**-eroong*

I didn't know there was a speed limit
Ich wußte nicht, daß es eine Höchstgeschwindigkeit gibt
*ikh **voos**-te nikht das es ine-e **hur'kst**-ge**shvin**-dikh-kite gipt*

How much is the fine?
Wieviel Strafe muß ich zahlen?
*vee**feel shtrah**-fe moos ikh **tsah**-len*

Where do I pay it?
Wo kann ich das bezahlen?
*voh kan ikh das be-**tsah**len*

Do I have to pay it straightaway?
Muß ich sofort bezahlen?
*moos ikh zo-**fort** be-**tsah**len*

I'm very sorry
Es tut mir sehr leid
es toot meer zayr lite

I would like to phone my embassy
Ich möchte mit meiner Botschaft telefonieren
*ikh mur'kh-te mit mine-er **boht**shaft taylay-fo-**nee**ren*

■ **YOU MAY HEAR**

Sie sind bei Rot über die Ampel gefahren
*zee zint by roht oober dee **am**pel ge-**fah**ren*
You went through a red light

■ **BODY** ■ **DOCTOR**

Larger towns usually have magazines listing cultural and political events and TV programmes.

What is there to do in the evenings?
Was kann man hier abends unternehmen?
*vas kan man heer **ah**-bents oonter-**nay**men*

Do you have a list of events for this month?
Haben Sie einen Veranstaltungskalender für diesen Monat?
*hah-ben zee ine-en fer-**an**shtal-toongs-kal**end**er foor deezen **moh**nat*

Is there anything for children?
Gibt es Veranstaltungen für Kinder?
*gipt es fer-**an**shtal-toongen foor **kin**der*

Where can I get tickets?
Wo kann ich Karten kaufen?
*vo kan ikh **kar**-ten kowfen*

for tonight
für heute abend
*foor **hoy**-te ahbent*

for the show
für die Show
foor dee shoh

for the football match
für das Fußballspiel
*foor das **foos**-ball-shpeel*

I'd like ... tickets
Ich möchte ... Karten
*ikh mur'kh-te ... **kar**-ten*

...adults
...Erwachsene
*...er**vak**-se-ne*

...children
...Kinder
*...**kin**der*

Where can we go dancing?
Wo kann man hier tanzen gehen?
*voh kan man heer **tan**tsen gayen*

What time does it open?
Wann macht das auf?
van makht das owf

How much is it to get in?
Was kostet der Eintritt?
*vas koset der **ine**-trit*

What is there to do here at weekends?
Was macht man hier am Wochenende?
*vas makht man heer am **vo**khen-**en**-de*

■ CINEMA ■ SIGHTSEEING & TOURIST OFFICE ■ THEATRE

To send a fax from the UK, the international codes for Germany are **010 49** (for what was West Germany) and **010 37** (for what was East Germany), followed by the German area code, e.g. Bonn **228**, Munich **89**, and then the number you require.

ADDRESSING A FAX	
TO	AN
FROM	VON
DATE	DATUM
RE:	BETREFF:
PLEASE FIND ATTACHED A COPY OF...	IN DER ANLAGE EINE KOPIE VON...
...PAGES IN TOTAL	...SEITEN INSGESAMT

I want to send a fax
Ich möchte ein Fax schicken
ikh mur'kh-te ine fax shicken

Do you have a fax?
Haben Sie ein Fax?
hah-ben zee ine fax

What is your fax number?
Wie ist Ihre Faxnummer?
vee ist ee-re fax-noomer

I am having trouble getting through to your fax
Ich komme bei Ihrem Fax nicht durch
ikh ko-me by ee-rem fax nikht doorkh

Please resend your fax
Bitte schicken Sie Ihr Fax noch einmal
bi-te shicken zee eer fax nokh ine-mal

I can't read it
Ich kann es nicht lesen
ikh kan es nikht lay-zen

Your fax is constantly engaged
Ihr Fax ist immer besetzt
eer fax ist immer bezetst

Can I send a fax from here?
Kann ich von hier ein Fax schicken?
kan ikh fon heer ine fax shicken

■ LETTERS ■ TELEPHONE

biscuits	die Kekse	*kek-se*
bread	das Brot	*broht*
bread (brown)	das Vollkornbrot	*folkorn-broht*
bread roll	das Brötchen	*brur't-khen*
butter	die Butter	*booter*
cereal	die Getreideflocken	*getry-de-flockhen*
cheese	der Käse	*kay-ze*
coffee (instant)	der Pulverkaffee	*poolfer-kafay*
cream	die Sahne	*zah-ne*
crisps	die Chips	*chips*
eggs	die Eier	*eye-er*
flour	das Mehl	*mayl*
ham	der Schinken	*shinken*
herbal tea	der Kräutertee	*krowter-tay*
honey	der Honig	*hohnikh*
jam	die Marmelade	*mar-melah-de*
margarine	die Margarine	*marga-ree-ne*
marmalade	die Orangenmarmelade	*oronjen-mar-melah-de*
milk	die Milch	*milkh*
mustard	der Senf	*zenf*
oil	das Öl	*ur'l*
orange juice	der Orangensaft	*oron-jen-zaft*
pasta	die Teigwaren	*tike-vahren*
pepper	der Pfeffer	*pfeffer*
rice	der Reis	*rice*
saccharin	der Süßstoff	*zoos-shtof*
salt	das Salz	*zalts*
sausage	die Wurst	*voorst*
stock cube	der Suppenwürfel	*zoo-pen-vur'-fel*
sugar	der Zucker	*tsooker*
tea	der Tee	*tay*
tin of tomatoes	die Dose Tomaten	*doh-ze tomah-ten*
vinegar	der Essig	*essikh*
yoghurt	der Joghurt	*yoh-goort*

■ **FRUIT**

apples	die Äpfel	*ep*fel
apricots	die Aprikosen	apri-**koh**-zen
bananas	die Bananen	*bana*-nen
cherries	die Kirschen	*keershen*
grapefruit	die Grapefruit	*grapefruit*
grapes	die Trauben	*trowben*
lemon	die Zitrone	tsi**troh**-ne
melon	die Melone	me**loh**-ne
nectarines	die Nektarinen	nek-ta-**ree**nen
oranges	die Orangen	o**ron**-jen
peaches	die Pfirsiche	**pfir**-zi-khe
pears	die Birnen	*bir*-nen
pineapple	die Ananas	*ananas*
plums	die Pflaumen	**pflow**-men
raspberries	die Himbeeren	**him**-bayren
strawberries	die Erdbeeren	**ert**-bayren
watermelon	die Wassermelone	**va**sser-me**loh**-ne

■ **VEGETABLES**

asparagus	der Spargel	**shpar**gel
carrots	die Karotten	ka-**rot**en
cauliflower	der Blumenkohl	**bloo**men-kohl
courgettes	die Zucchini	tsoo-**kee**nee
French beans	die grünen Bohnen	*groonen bohnen*
garlic	der Knoblauch	**knohp**-lowkh
leeks	der Lauch	*lowkh*
lettuce	der Kopfsalat	**kopf**-zalaht
mushrooms	die Pilze	*pilt*-se
onions	die Zwiebeln	**tsvee**beln
peas	die Erbsen	*erp*sen
peppers	die Paprikaschote	**pa**preeka-shoh-te
potatoes	die Kartoffeln	kar-**tof**eln
spinach	der Spinat	shpi**naht**
tomatoes	die Tomaten	to**mah**-ten

*In southern Germany and Austria you often hear the greeting **Grüß Gott** for **hello**. In Switzerland you will hear **Gruezi** for **hello** and **Ade** for **goodbye**.*

Hello!
Hallo! / Grüß Gott
ha**lo** / groos got

Goodbye!
Auf Wiedersehen
owf **vee**der-zayn

Hello
Guten Tag (used all day)
gooten tahk

Hi!
Hi!
hi

Bye!
Tschüs
tshoos

Good morning
Guten Morgen
gooten **mor**gen

Good evening
Guten Abend
gooten **ah**bent

Good night
Gute Nacht
goo-te nakht

Pleased to meet you
Angenehm
an-genaym

It's a pleasure
Freut mich
froyt mikh

How are you?
Wie geht's?
vee gayts

Fine, thanks
Danke, gut
dang-ke goot

And you?
Und Ihnen?
oont **ee**-nen

See you tomorrow
Bis morgen
bis **mor**gen

See you soon
Bis bald
bis balt

■ BASICS ■ MAKING FRIENDS

These phrases are intended for use at the hotel desk. More details about rooms can be found in the ACCOMMODATION topic.

Do you have a room for tonight?
Haben Sie ein Zimmer für heute nacht?
*hah-ben zee ine **tsi**mmer foor **hoy**-te nakht*

I booked a room in the name of...
Ich habe ein Zimmer auf den Namen ... reserviert
*ikh **hah**-be ine **tsi**mmer owf den **nah**-men ... ray-zer-**veert***

I'd like to see the room
Ich möchte das Zimmer gerne ansehen
*ikh mur'kh-te das **tsi**mmer gern-e an-**zay**en*

Have you another?
Haben Sie noch ein anderes?
*hah-ben zee nokh ine **an**-de-res*

Where can I park the car?
Wo kann ich mein Auto parken?
*voh kan ich mine **ow**to **par**ken*

What time is...?	**dinner** (evening)	**breakfast**
Wann gibt es...?	Abendessen	Frühstück
van gipt es...	*ah**bent-essen*	*froo-shtook*

We'll be back late tonight
Wir kommen heute abend spät zurück
*veer kommen **hoy**-te **ah**bent shpayt tsoo**rook***

The key, please	**Room number...**
Den Schlüssel, bitte	Zimmer (number)...
*den **shloo**-sel **bi**-te*	*tsi**mmer...*

Are there any messages for me?
Sind Nachrichten für mich da?
*zint **nahkh**-rikhten foor mikh dah*

I'm leaving tomorrow	**Please prepare the bill**
Ich reise morgen ab	Machen Sie bitte die Rechnung fertig
*ikh **ry**-ze **mor**gen ab*	*makhen zee **bi**-te dee **rekh**-noong **fer**tikh*

■ ACCOMMODATION ■ ROOM SERVICE

*With the Single European Market, goods within the EC are allowed to travel freely. Businesses supplying goods to VAT-registered EC companies are required to complete a Sales List which accompanies the goods. The VAT (**MWST**) registration code for Germany is **DE** followed by the German company's 9-digit number. VAT is paid at the rate of the destination country.*

What is your VAT registered number?
Wie ist Ihre Mehrwertsteuernummer?
*vee ist ee-re **mayr**-vayrt-shtoyer-**noo**mer*

Our VAT number is... *(GB followed by number)*
Unsere Mehrwertsteuernummer ist...
***oon**-ze-re **mayr**-vayrt-shtoyer-**noo**mer ist...*

Please deliver the goods to...
Bitte liefern Sie die Waren an...
***bi**-te **lee**fern zee dee **vah**ren an...*

The consignment must be accompanied by a pro forma invoice
Den Waren muß eine Pro-Forma-Rechnung beiliegen
*den **vah**ren moos ine-e proh-**for**ma-rekh-noong **by**-leegen*

How long will it take to deliver?
Wie lange dauert die Lieferung?
*vee lang-e **dow**-ert dee **lee**-feroong*

Delivery will take ... days / weeks
Die Lieferung braucht ... Tage / Wochen
*dee **lee**-feroong browkht ... **tah**-ge / **vo**-khen*

Please fax a copy of the pro forma invoice
Bitte faxen Sie mir eine Kopie der Pro-Forma-Rechnung
***bi**-te faxen zee meer ine-e ko**pee** der proh-**for**ma-rekh-noong*

Please confirm safe delivery of the goods
Bitte bestätigen Sie den ordnungsgemäßen Eingang der Waren
***bi**-te be-**shtay**-tigen zee den **ord**noonks-ge-**may**sen **ine**-gang der **vah**ren*

■ NUMBERS ■ OFFICE

REINIGUNG	DRY-CLEANER'S
AUTOMATENWASCHSALON	LAUNDERETTE
WASCHPULVER	WASHING POWDER

Where can I do some washing?
Wo kann ich hier Wäsche waschen?
*voh kan ikh heer **ve**-she vashen*

Can I have my laundry washed here?
Kann ich hier Wäsche waschen lassen?
*kan ikh heer **ve**-she vashen lassen*

When will my things be ready?
Wann sind meine Sachen fertig?
*van zint mine-e **zakh**-en **fer**tikh*

Where is the nearest launderette?
Wo ist der nächste Automatenwaschsalon?
*voh ist der **nekh**-ste owto-**mah**ten-vash-sa**long***

Where is the nearest dry-cleaner's?
Wo ist die nächste Reinigung?
*voh ist dee **nekh**-ste **ry**-nigoong*

What coins do I need?
Was für Münzen brauche ich?
*vas foor **moon**-tsen **brow**-khe ikh*

Is there somewhere I can dry my clothes?
Kann ich hier irgendwo Sachen zum Trocknen aufhängen?
*kan ikh heer ir-gent-voh **zakh**-en tsoom **trok**nen **owf**-hengen*

Can you iron this for me?
Könnten Sie das für mich bügeln?
***kur'n**-ten zee das foor mikh **boo**geln*

Can I borrow an iron?
Kann ich ein Bügeleisen haben?
*kan ikh ine **boo**gel-ize-en **hah**-ben*

■ **ROOM SERVICE**

51

Where can I/we...?
Wo kann man hier...?
voh kan man heer...

go fishing
gut angeln
goot angeln

go riding
gut reiten
goot ry-ten

Are there any good beaches near here?
Sind hier in der Nähe gute Strände?
sint heer in der nay-e goo-te shtren-de

Is there a swimming pool near here?
Gibt es ein Freibad *(outdoor)* / Hallenbad *(indoor)* in der Nähe?
gipt es ine fry-baht / hallen-baht in der nay-e

Where can I/we hire bikes?
Wo kann man Fahrräder leihen?
voh kan man fah-rehder lye-en

Do you have cycling helmets?
Haben Sie Sturzhelme für Radfahrer?
hah-ben zee shtoorts-helm-e foor rat-fahrer

How much is it...?
Was kostet das...?
vas kostet das...

per hour
pro Stunde
pro shtoon-de

per day
am Tag
am tahk

What do you do in your spare time? *(familiar)*
Was machst du in deiner Freizeit?
vas makhst doo in dine-er fry-tsite

I like gardening
Ich arbeite gern im Garten
ikh ar-by-te gern im garten

I like photography
Ich fotografiere gern
ikh fotogra-fee-re gern

I like playing...
Ich spiele gern...
ikh shpee-le gern...

tennis
Tennis
tennis

football
Fußball
foos-ball

Do you like playing...?
Spielen Sie gerne...?
shpeelen zee gern-e...

Do you like playing...? *(familiar)*
Spielst du gerne...?
shpeelst doo gern-e...

■ CINEMA ■ MUSIC ■ SPORTS ■ TELEVISION ■ WALKING

17 May 1994	17. Mai 1994
Dear Sir / Madam	Sehr geehrte Damen und Herren *(Sie)*
Yours faithfully	Mit freundlichen Grüßen
Dear Mr...	Sehr geehrter Herr.... *(Sie)*
Dear Mrs...	Sehr geehrte Frau.... *(Sie)*
Yours sincerely	Mit freundlichen Grüßen
Dear Christian	Lieber Christian *(Sie)*
Dear Petra	Liebe Petra *(Sie)*
Best regards	Mit besten Grüßen
Dear ...	Lieber / Liebe... *(du)*
Love	Mit herzlichen Grüßen

Further to your letter of 7 May...
Mit Bezug auf Ihr Schreiben vom 7. Mai...

Further to our telephone conversation...
Im Anschluß an unser Telefongespräch...

Please find enclosed...
In der Anlage finden Sie...

Thank you for the information / for your price list
Vielen Dank für die Information / für Ihre Preisliste

I look forward to hearing from you soon
Ich freue mich auf Ihre baldige Antwort

by return [of] post
postwendend

■ FAX ■ OFFICE

53

*You often need a coin (I DM or 2 DM) to unlock the trolley, so
make sure you have some small change on arrival.*

GEPÄCKAUSGABE	BAGGAGE RECLAIM
GEPÄCKAUFBEWAHRUNG	LEFT-LUGGAGE OFFICE
SCHLIESSFACH	LEFT-LUGGAGE LOCKER

My luggage isn't there
Mein Gepäck ist nicht da
*mine ge**pek** ist nikht dah*

My suitcase has been damaged on the flight
Mein Koffer wurde beim Flug beschädigt
*mine kofer voor-de bime flook be-**shay**-dikht*

What has happened to the luggage on the flight from...?
Was ist mit dem Gepäck vom Flug aus...?
*vas ist mit dem ge**pek** fom flook ows...*

Can you help me with my luggage, please?
Könnten Sie mir bitte mit meinem Gepäck helfen?
***kur'n**-ten zee meer **bi**-te mit mine-em ge**pek** helfen*

When does the left luggage office open / close?
Wann macht die Gepäckaufbewahrung auf / zu?
*van makht dee ge**pek**-**owf**-bevah-roong owf / tsoo*

We'd like to leave this overnight
Wir möchten das über Nacht aufgeben
*veer mur'kh-ten das oober nakht **owf**-geben*

Can I leave my luggage here?
Kann ich mein Gepäck hierlassen?
*kan ikh mine ge**pek** **heer**-lassen*

I'll collect it at...
Ich hole es um ... Uhr ab
*ikh **hoh**-le es oom ... oor ap*

■ YOU MAY HEAR

Sie können es bis sechs Uhr da lassen
*zee **kur'**-nen es bis zekhs oor **dah** lassen*
You may leave it here until 6 o'clock

■ AIR TRAVEL

*We have used the familiar **du** form for these questions.*

What's your name?
Wie heißt du?
vee hyst doo

My name is...
Ich heiße...
*ikh **hy**-se...*

How old are you?
Wie alt bist du?
vee alt bist doo

I'm ... years old
Ich bin ... Jahre alt
*ikh bin ... **yah**-re alt*

Are you from Germany?
Bist du aus Deutschland?
*bist doo ows **doytch**-lant*

I'm English *(I come from...)*
Ich komme aus England
*ikh **ko**-me ows **eng**-lant*

Where do you live?
Wo wohnst du?
voh vohnst doo

Where do you live? *(plural)*
Wo wohnt ihr?
voh vohnt eer

I live in London
Ich wohne in London
*ikh **voh**-ne in **lon**don*

We live in Glasgow
Wir wohnen in Glasgow
*veer vohnen in **glas**gow*

I'm still studying
Ich studiere noch
*ikh shtoo-**dee**-re nokh*

I work
Ich arbeite
*ikh **ar**-by-te*

I'm retired
Ich bin pensioniert
*ikh bin penzyoh-**neert***

I'm... **(not) married**
Ich bin... (nicht) verheiratet
*ikh bin... (nikht) fer-**hy**rah-tet*

divorced
geschieden
*ge-**shee**den*

widow(er)
Witwe(r)
***vit**-ve(r)*

I have... **a boyfriend**
Ich habe... einen Freund
*ikh **hah**-be... ine-en froynt*

a girlfriend
eine Freundin
*ine-e **froyn**-din*

I have ... children
Ich habe ... Kinder
*ikh **hah**-be ... **kin**der*

I have no children
Ich habe keine Kinder
*ikh **hah**-be kine-e **kin**der*

I'm here on holiday
Ich bin hier auf Urlaub
*ikh bin heer owf **oor**lowp*

I'm here on business
Ich bin geschäftlich hier
*ikh bin ge**sheft**-likh heer*

■ LEISURE/INTERESTS ■ SPORTS ■ WEATHER ■ WORK

Large railway stations and airport bookshops usually stock English newspapers and books, but they can be very expensive.

Have you...?   **a map of the town / a map of the region**
Haben Sie...?   einen Stadtplan / eine Karte der Umgebung
hah-ben zee...   *ine-en shtat-plan / ine-e kar-te oom-gayboong*

Can you show me where ... is on the map?
Können Sie mir auf der Karte zeigen, wo ... ist?
kur'-nen zee meer owf der kar-te tsy-gen, voh ... ist

Do you have a more detailed map of the area?
Haben Sie eine genauere Karte der Gegend?
hah-ben zee ine-e ge-nower-e kar-te der gaygent

Can you draw me a map?
Können Sie mir einen Plan zeichnen?
kur'-nen zee meer ine-en plan tsykh-nen

Do you have a guide book / a leaflet in English?
Gibt es einen Reiseführer / eine Broschüre auf Englisch?
gipt es ine-en ry-ze-foorer / ine-e bro-shoo-re owf eng-lish

Could I have this in English?
Könnte ich das auf Englisch haben?
kur'n-te ikh das owf eng-lish hah-ben

Where can I/we buy an English newspaper?
Wo kann man englische Zeitungen kaufen?
voh kan man english-e tsy-toongen kowfen

Do you have any English newspapers / novels?
Haben Sie englische Zeitungen / Bücher?
hah-ben zee english-e tsy-toongen / boo-kher

When do the English newspapers arrive?
Wann kommen die englischen Zeitungen an?
van kommen dee english-en tsy-toongen an

Please put *(name newspaper)* **aside for me**
Bitte legen Sie für mich ... zurück
bi-te laygen zee foor mikh ... tsoorook

■ **DIRECTIONS** ■ **SIGHTSEEING & TOURIST OFFICE**

■ LIQUIDS

1/2 litre (c.1 pint)	einen halben Liter	ine-en halben leeter
a litre of...	einen Liter...	ine-en leeter...
a bottle of...	eine Flasche...	ine-e **fla**-she...
a glass of...	ein Glas...	ine glahs...
a small glass	ein kleines Glas	ine **kline**-es glahs
a large glass	ein großes Glas	ine **groh**-ses glahs

■ WEIGHTS

100 grams of...	hundert Gramm...	**hoon**dert gram...
a pound (=500 g)	ein Pfund	ine pfoont
a kilo of...	ein Kilo...	ine keelo...

■ FOOD

a slice of...	eine Scheibe...	ine-e shy-be...
a portion of...	eine Portion...	ine-e por-**tsyohn**...
a dozen...	ein Dutzend...	ine **doo**-tsent...
a packet of...	ein Paket...	ine pa**kayt**...
a tin of...	eine Dose...	ine-e **doh**-ze...
a jar of...	ein Glas...	ine glahs...

■ MISCELLANEOUS

10 Marks worth of...	für zehn Mark...	foor tsayn mark...
a third	ein Drittel	ine drittel
a quarter	ein Viertel	ine feertel
ten per cent	zehn Prozent	tsayn pro-**tsent**
more...	noch etwas...	nokh **et**vas...
less...	weniger...	**vayni**-ger...
enough	genug	ge-**nook**
double	doppelt	dop-elt
twice	zweimal	**tsvy**-mal
three times	dreimal	**dry**-mal

■ FOOD ■ SHOPPING

*In many cities you can get **eine Touristenkarte** (which covers all public transport), or **eine Familienkarte** (2 adults, 2 children). Ask for **spezielle Fahrkarten**. Usually there is a zone system and you will be asked if you want a card for **die Innenstadt** (inner city) or for **das gesamte Stadtgebiet** (all zones).*

Where is the nearest metro station?
Wo ist die nächste U-Bahn-Haltestelle?
*voh ist dee **nay**-kste **oo**bahn-hal-te-shte-le*

How does the ticket machine work?
Wie funktioniert der Automat?
*vee foonk-tsyoh-**neert** der owto-**maht***

I'm going to...
Ich möchte nach...
ikh mur'kh-te nakh...

Do you have a map of the metro?
Gibt es eine Karte mit allen U-Bahn-Linien?
*gipt es ine-e kar-te mit **a**-len **oo**-bahn-**lee**-nee-en*

How do I get to...?
Wie komme ich nach...?
*vee **ko**-me ikh nakh...*

Do I have to change?
Muß ich umsteigen?
*moos ikh **oom**-shtygen*

Where?
Wo?
voh

Which line is it for...?
Welche Linie fährt nach...?
***vel**-khe **lee**-nee-e fayrt nakh...*

In which direction?
In welche Richtung?
*in **vel**-khe **rikh**toong*

What is the next stop?
Was ist der nächste Halt?
*vas ist der **nehk**-ste halt*

May I get past?
Darf ich mal vorbei, bitte?
*darf ikh mal for-**by** bi-te*

I have to get our here
Ich muß hier aussteigen
*ikh moos heer **ows**-shtygen*

■ YOU MAY HEAR

Für welche Zonen?
*foor **vel**-khe **tsoh**-nen*
For which zones?

Für die Innenstadt?
*foor dee **inn**en-shtat*
For the city centre?

■ BUS ■ TAXI

*You can change money and traveller's cheques where you see the sign **Geldwechsel**. Cash dispensers usually let you choose which language to carry out the transaction in. However, in smaller places, you might have trouble finding one that takes your card.*

Where can I change some money?
Wo kann ich hier Geld wechseln?
*voh kan ikh heer gelt **vek**-seln*

I want to change these traveller's cheques
Ich würde gerne diese Reiseschecks einlösen
*ikh **voor**-de gern-e dee-ze **ry**-ze-sheks **ine**-lur'-zen*

When does the bank open?
Wann macht die Bank auf?
van makht dee bank owf

When does the bank close?
Wann macht die Bank zu?
van makht dee bank tsoo

Can I pay with pounds / dollars?
Kann ich in Pfund / Dollar bezahlen?
*kan ikh in pfoont / dollar be**tsah**-len*

Can I use my credit card to get Marks?
Kann ich hier mit meiner Kreditkarte D-Mark bekommen?
*kan ikh heer mit mine-er kre**deet**-kar-te **day**-mark be-**ko**mmen*

Can I use my card with this cash dispenser?
Kann ich an diesem Geldautomaten meine Kreditkarte benutzen? *kan ikh an deezem **gelt**-owto-**mah**ten mine-e kre**deet**-kar-te be**noot**sen*

The cash dispenser has swallowed my credit card
Der Geldautomat hat meine Kreditkarte geschluckt
*der **gelt**-owto-maht hat mine-e kre**deet**-kar-te ge-**shlookt***

Have you any change?
Haben Sie Kleingeld?
*hah-ben zee **kline**-gelt*

■ PAYING

Are there any good concerts on in the next few days?
Sind gute Konzerte in der nächsten Zeit?
zint goo-te kon-tser-te in der nehk-sten tsite

Where can I/we get tickets for the concert?
Wo gibt es Karten für das Konzert?
voh gipt es kar-ten foor das kon-tsert

Where can I/we hear some classical music / jazz?
Wo kann man hier klassische Musik / Jazz hören?
voh kan man heer klas-sish-e moozeek / jazz hur'-en

What sort of music do you like?   **I like...**
Welche Musik mögen Sie?   Ich mag...
vel-khe moozeek mur'gen zee   *ikh mahk...*

Which is your favourite group? *(familiar)*
Was ist deine Lieblingsgruppe?
vas ist dine-e leeplings-groop-e

Who is your favourite singer? *(familiar)*
Wer ist dein Lieblingssänger?
ver ist dine dine leeplings-zenger

Can you play any musical instruments? *(familiar)*
Spielst du ein Instrument?
shpeelst doo ine in-stroo-ment

I play...	**the guitar**	**piano**	**clarinet**
Ich spiele...	Gitarre	Klavier	Klarinette
ikh shpee-le...	*gee-ta-re*	*kla-veer*	*klari-net-te*

Have you been to any good concerts recently? *(familiar)*
Warst du in letzter Zeit in einem guten Konzert?
vahrst doo in lets-ter tsite in ine-em gooten kon-tsert

Do you like opera?   **Do you like reggae?** *(familiar)*
Mögen Sie Oper?   Magst du Reggae?
mur'gen zee oh-per   *mahkst doo reggae*

■ ENTERTAINMENT ■ MAKING FRIENDS

0	null	*nool*	1st	erste	*er-ste*
1	eins	*ines*			
2	zwei	*tsvy*	2nd	zweite	*tsvy-te*
3	drei	*dry*			
4	vier	*feer*	3rd	dritte	*drit-te*
5	fünf	*foonf*			
6	sechs	*zekhs*	4th	vierte	*feer-te*
7	sieben	*zee*ben			
8	acht	*akht*	5th	fünfte	*foonf-te*
9	neun	*noyn*			
10	zehn	*tsayn*	6th	sechste	*zehks-te*
11	elf	*elf*			
12	zwölf	*tsvur'lf*	7th	siebte	*zeep-te*
13	dreizehn	*dry-tsayn*			
14	vierzehn	*feer-tsayn*	8th	achte	*akh-te*
15	fünfzehn	*foonf-tsayn*			
16	sechzehn	*zekh-tsayn*	9th	neunte	*noyn-te*
17	siebzehn	*zeep-tsayn*			
18	achtzehn	*akh-tsayn*	10th	zehnte	*tsayn-te*
19	neunzehn	*noyn-tsayn*			
20	zwanzig	*tsvan-tsikh*			
21	einundzwanzig	*ine-oont-tsvan-tsikh*			
22	zweiundzwanzig	*tsvy-oont-tsvan-tsikh*			
23	dreiundzwanzig	*dry-oont-tsvan-tsikh*			
24	vierundzwanzig	*feer-oont-tsvan-tsikh*			
25	fünfundzwanzig	*foonf-oont-tsvan-tsikh*			
26	sechsundzwanzig	*zekhs-ont-tsvan-tsikh*			
27	siebenundzwanzig	*zee*ben-ont-tsvan-tsikh			
28	achtundzwanzig	*akht-ont-tsvan-tsikh*			
29	neunundzwanzig	*noyn-oont-tsvan-tsikh*			
30	dreißig	*dry-sikh*			
40	vierzig	*feer-tsikh*			
50	fünfzig	*foonf-tsikh*			
60	sechzig	*zekh-tsikh*			
70	siebzig	*zeep-tsikh*			
80	achtzig	*akh-tsikh*			
90	neunzig	*noyn-tsikh*			
100	hundert	*hoon*dert			
101	hunderteins	*hoon*dert-ines			
200	zweihundert	*tsvy-hoondert*			
1,000	tausend	*tow*zent			
2,000	zweitausend	*tsvy-towzent*			
1 million	eine Million	*ine-e milyohn*			

AN APPOINTMENT	EIN TERMIN
EXTENSION...	APPARAT...
SWITCHBOARD	DIE VERMITTLUNG

I'd like to speak to the office manager
Ich möchte bitte den Chef / die Chefin sprechen
*ikh mur'kh-te **bi**-te den shef / dee shefin **shpre**-khen*

What is your address?
Wie ist Ihre Adresse?
*vee ist ee-re a-**dre**-se*

Which floor?
Welches Stockwerk?
*vel-khes **shtok**verk*

Can you photocopy this for me?
Könnten Sie das für mich photokopieren?
***kur'n**-ten zee das foor mikh foto-ko**pee**-ren*

Do you use a courier service?
Benutzen Sie einen Kurierdienst?
*be**noot**sen zee ine-en koo-**reer**-deenst*

Can you send this for me?
Könnten Sie das für mich mit Kurier schicken?
***kur'n**-ten zee das foor mikh mit koo-**reer** shicken*

When does the office open?
Wann macht das Büro auf?
*van makht das boo**roh** owf*

When does the office close?
Wann macht das Büro zu?
*van makht das boo**roh** tsoo*

How do I find your office?
Wie finde ich Ihr Büro?
*vee **fin**-de ikh eer boo**roh***

■ **YOU MAY HEAR**

Bitte nehmen Sie schon einmal Platz
***bi**-te naymen zee shur'n **ine**-mal plats*
Please take a seat

Ich komme sofort
*ikh **ko**-me zo-**fort***
I will be with you in just a moment

■ **BUSINESS–MEETING** ■ **FAX** ■ **LETTERS**

AMOUNT TO BE PAID	DER BETRAG
BILL	DIE RECHNUNG
CASH DESK	DIE KASSE
RECEIPT	DIE QUITTUNG

How much is it?
Was kostet das?
vas kostet das

Can I pay...?
Kann ich ... bezahlen?
*kan ikh ... be**tsah**-len*

by credit card
mit Kreditkarte
*mit kre**deet**-kar-te*

by cheque
mit Scheck
mit shek

Do you take credit cards?
Nehmen Sie Kreditkarten?
*naymen zee kre**deet**-karten*

Is service / VAT included?
Ist die Bedienung / die Mehrwertsteuer inbegriffen?
*ist dee be-**dee**noong / dee **mayr**-vayrt-shtoy-er **in**-be-griffen*

Put it on my bill
Setzen Sie es auf meine Rechnung
***zet**-sen zee es owf mine-e **rekh**-noong*

Could I have a receipt, please?
Könnte ich eine Quittung haben, bitte?
***kur'n**-te ikh ine-e **kvi**-toong **hah**-ben **bi**-te*

Do I have to pay in advance?
Muß ich im voraus zahlen?
*moos ikh im for-**ows** tsah-len*

Do you require a deposit?
Nehmen Sie eine Kaution?
*naymen zee ine-e kow-**tsyohn***

I'm sorry
Tut mir leid
toot meer lite

I've nothing smaller
Ich habe es nicht kleiner
*ikh **hah**-be es nikht kline-er*

Keep the change
Stimmt so
shtimt zoh

■ MONEY ■ SHOPPING

SUPER	4 STAR
BLEIFREI	UNLEADED
DIESEL	DIESEL
BENZIN	PETROL
SELBSTBEDIENUNG	SELF-SERVICE

Is there a petrol station near here?
Ist hier in der Nähe eine Tankstelle?
*ist heer in der **nay**-e ine-e **tank**-shte-le*

Fill it up, please
Volltanken, bitte
*fol-tang-ken **bi**-te*

Please check the oil / the water
Bitte überprüfen Sie das Öl / das Wasser
*bi-te oober-**proo**fen zee das ur'l / das vasser*

...DM worth of unleaded petrol
Für ... DM bleifrei bitte
*foor ... day-mark **bly**-fry **bi**-te*

Where is...?
Wo ist...?
voh ist...

the air line
die Druckluft
dee drook-looft

the water
das Wasser
das vasser

Please check the tyre pressure
Bitte überprüfen Sie den Reifendruck
*bi-te oober-**proo**fen zee den **ry**fen-drook*

Can you fill this can with petrol, please?
Könnten Sie diesen Kanister mit Benzin füllen?
*kur'n-ten zee deezen ka-**nister** mit bent**seen foo**len*

Do you take this credit card?
Nehmen Sie diese Kreditkarte?
*naymen zee dee-ze kre**deet**-kar-te*

Where do I pay?
Wo kann ich zahlen?
*voh kan ikh **tsah**-len*

■ **YOU MAY HEAR**

Welche Säule?
***vel**-khe **soy**-le*
Which pump?

■ **BREAKDOWNS** ■ **CAR**

APOTHEKE	PHARMACY
DIENSTHABENDE APOTHEKE	DUTY CHEMIST
REZEPT	PRESCRIPTION

I don't feel well
Ich fühle mich nicht wohl
ikh foo-le mikh nikht vohl

Have you something for...?
Haben Sie etwas gegen...?
hah-ben zee etvas gay-gen...

a headache
Kopfschmerzen
kopf-shmertsen

car sickness
Reisekrankheit
ry-ze-krank-hite

diarrhoea
Durchfall
doorkh-fal

I have a rash
Ich habe einen Ausschlag
ikh hah-be ine-en ows-shlahk

Is it safe to give children?
Kann man es bedenkenlos auch Kindern geben?
kan man es be-deng-ken-lohs owkh kindern gayben

■ YOU MAY HEAR

Dreimal täglich vor dem / beim / nach dem Essen
dry-mal tayk-likh for dem / bime / nakh dem essen
Three times a day before / with / after meals

■ WORDS YOU MAY NEED

antiseptic	das Antiseptikum	anti-zepti-koom
aspirin	das Aspirin	aspi-reen
cold	die Erkältung	er-keltoong
condoms	die Kondome	kondom-e
cotton wool	die Watte	va-te
dental floss	die Zahnseide	tsahn-zy-de
plasters	die Pflaster	pflaster
sanitary pads	die Binden	binden
sore throat	die Halsschmerzen	halts-shmertsen
tampons	die Tampons	tampons
toothpaste	die Zahnpasta	tsahn-pasta

■ BODY ■ DOCTOR

65

Tapes for video cameras and camcorders can be bought in photographic shops, department stores and hypermarkets.

Where can I buy tapes for a video camera?
Wo kann man Videobänder für eine Videokamera kaufen?
*voh kan man **vee**day-o-bender foor ine-e **vee**day-o-kamera kowfen*

A colour film   **with 24 / 36 exposures**
Einen Farbfilm   mit 24 / 36 Bildern
*ine-en **farp**-film   mit **feer**-oont-tsvan-tsikh / **zekh**s-oont-drysikh **bil**dern*

A video tape for this video camera
Ein Videoband für diese Videokamera
*ine **vee**day-o-bant foor dee-ze **vee**day-o-kamera*

Have you batteries...?   **for this camera / videocamera**
Haben Sie Batterien...?   für diese Kamera / Videokamera
***hah**-ben zee ba-te**ree**-en...?   foor dee-ze kamera / **vee**day-o-kamera*

Can you develop this film?   **How much will it be?**
Können Sie diesen Film entwickeln?   Was kostet das?
***kur'**-nen zee deezen film ent**vi**-keln   *vas kostet das*

Matt / Glossy, please
Matt / Hochglanz, bitte
*mat / **hohkh**-glants **bi**-te*

When will the photos be ready?
Wann sind die Fotos fertig?
*van zint dee **fo**tos **fer**tikh*

The film is stuck   **Can you take it out, please?**
Der Film klemmt   Können Sie ihn bitte herausnehmen?
*der film klemt   **kur'**-nen zee een **bi**-te her**ows**-naymen*

Is it OK to take pictures here?
Darf man hier fotografieren?
*darf man heer foto-gra-**fee**ren*

Would you take a picture of us, please?
Könnten Sie bitte ein Bild von uns machen?
***kur'n**-ten zee **bi**-te ein bilt fon oons **ma**khen*

■ **SHOPPING**

Main Post Offices are open all day Mon.-Fri. and on Saturday mornings. A red dot on German postboxes indicates that there is a late/weekend collection.

POST OFFICE	**DAS POSTAMT / DIE POST**
POSTBOX	**DER BRIEFKASTEN**
STAMPS	**DIE BRIEFMARKEN**

Where is the nearest post office?
Wo ist das nächste Postamt?
*voh ist das **nekh**-ste **post**amt*

When is it open?
Wann hat es auf?
van hat es owf

Is there a postbox near here?
Ist ein Briefkasten in der Nähe?
*ist ine **breef**-kasten in der **nay**-e*

Where can I buy stamps?
Wo bekomme ich Briefmarken?
*voh be-**ko**-me ikh **breef**-marken*

Stamps for ... postcards to Great Britain, please
Briefmarken für ... Postkarten nach England, bitte
***breef**-marken foor ... **post**-karten nakh **eng**-lant **bi**-te*

I want to send this parcel to...
Ich möchte dieses Paket nach ... schicken
*ikh mur'kh-te deezes pa-**kayt** nakh ... shicken*

How much is it for this parcel?
Was kostet dieses Paket?
*vas kostet deezes pa**kayt***

by airmail
per Luftpost
*per **looft**post*

It's a gift
Es ist ein Geschenk
*es ist ine ge-**shenk***

The value is...
Der Wert ist...
der vayrt ist...

■ YOU MAY HEAR

Füllen Sie das bitte aus
foolen zee das bi-te ows
Fill in this form, please

■ DIRECTIONS

Can you help me?
Können Sie mir helfen?
kur'-nen zee meer helfen

I only speak a little German
Ich spreche nur sehr wenig Deutsch
ikh shpre-khe noor zayr venikh doytch

Does anyone here speak English?
Spricht hier jemand Englisch?
shprikht heer yaymant eng-lish

What's the matter?
Was ist los?
vas ist lohs

I have a problem
Ich habe ein Problem
ikh hah-be ine problem

I'm lost
Ich habe mich verlaufen *(on foot)*
ikh hah-be mikh fer-lowfen

How do I get to...?
Wie komme ich nach...?
vee ko-me ikh nakh...

I've missed...
Ich habe ... verpaßt
ikh hah-be ... fer-past

my plane
mein Flugzeug
mine flook-tsoyk

my connection
meinen Anschluß
mine-en an-shloos

My coach has left without me
Mein Bus ist ohne mich abgefahren
mine boos ist oh-ne mikh ap-gefahren

Can you show me how this works?
Können Sie mir zeigen, wie das geht?
kur'-nen zee meer tsy-gen vee das gayt

I have lost my money
Ich habe mein Geld verloren
ikh hah-be mine gelt fer-lohren

I need to get to...
Ich muß nach...
ikh moos nakh...

Is there a lost property office?
Gibt es hier ein Fundbüro?
gipt es heer ine foont-booroh

Where is it?
Wo ist es?
voh ist es

I need to phone the British consulate
Ich muß das britische Konsulat anrufen
ikh moos das british-e konsoo-laht an-roofen

Leave me alone!
Lassen Sie mich in Ruhe!
lassen zee mikh in roo-e

Go away!
Hau ab!
how ap

■ COMPLAINTS ■ EMERGENCIES

Do you have...?
Haben Sie...?
hah-ben zee...

When...?
Wann...?
van...

At what time...?
Um wieviel Uhr...?
oom veefeel oor...

Where is / are...?
Wo ist / sind...?
vo ist / sint...

Can I...?
Kann ich...?
kan ikh...

May we...?
Können wir bitte...?
kur'-nen veer bi-te...

Is it...?
Ist es...?
ist es...

Are they...?
Sind sie?
zint zee

Is / Are there...?
Gibt es...?
gipt es...

How far is it?
Wie weit ist?
vee vite ist

What time is it?
Wieviel Uhr ist es?
veefeel oor ist es

How much is that?
Was kostet das?
vas kostet das

Who are you?
Wer sind Sie?
vayr zint zee

Who...?
Wer...?
vayr...

What...?
Was...?
vas...

Why...?
Warum...?
vahroom...

How much...? / How many...?
Wieviel...? / Wie viele...?
veefeel... / vee fee-le...

How...?
Wie...?
vee...

Which one?
Welcher / Welche?
vel-kher / vel-khe

Where are the toilets?
Wo sind die Toiletten?
voh zint dee twa-le-ten

■ BASICS

SCHUHMACHER / SCHUSTER	SHOE REPAIR SHOP
SCHNELLREPARATUR	REPAIRS WHILE YOU WAIT

This is broken
Das ist kaputt
*das ist ka**poot***

Is it worth repairing?
Lohnt sich die Reparatur?
*lohnt zikh dee raypa-ra-**toor***

Can you repair...?
Können Sie ... reparieren?
***kur'**-nen zee ... raypa-**ree**ren*

Can you do it straightaway?
Können Sie das gleich machen?
***kur'**-nen zee das glykh **ma**khen*

How long will it take?
Wie lange dauert das?
*vee lang-e **dow**-ert das*

Where can I get this repaired?
Wo kann ich das reparieren lassen?
*voh kan ikh das raypa-**ree**ren lassen*

How much will it be?
Was kostet das?
vas kostet das

these shoes	my watch
diese Schuhe	meine Uhr
dee-ze shoo-e	*mine-e oor*

Can I wait?
Kann ich warten?
*kan ikh **var**-ten*

When will it be ready?
Wann ist es fertig?
*van ist es **fer**tikh*

Where can I have my shoes reheeled?
Wo kann ich neue Absätze an meine Schuhe machen lassen?
*voh kan ikh **noy**-e **ap**-zet-se an mine-e shoo-e **ma**khen lassen*

I need some glue
Ich brauche Uhu®
*ikh **brow**-khe **oo**-hoo*

I need some Sellotape®
Ich brauche Tesafilm®
*ikh **brow**-khe **tay**za-film*

Do you have a needle and thread?
Haben Sie Nadel und Faden?
***hah**-ben zee **nah**del oont **fah**den*

The fuse has blown
Die Sicherung ist raus
*dee **zikh**-eroong ist rows*

■ **BREAKDOWNS**

Come in!
Herein!
he-*rine*

Please come back later
Bitte kommen Sie später noch einmal
bi-te kommen zee shpayter nokh *ine*-mal

Can you bring me breakfast in my room?
Können Sie mir das Frühstück aufs Zimmer bringen?
kur'n-nen zee meer das *froo*-shtook owfs *tsi*mmer bringen

Please bring...
Bitte bringen Sie...
bi-te bringen zee...

a glass
ein Glas
ine glahs

clean towels
saubere Handtücher
zow-be-re *hant*-tookher

toilet paper
Toilettenpapier
twa-*le*-ten-pa*peer*

Could you wake me early tomorrow morning?
Können Sie mich bitte morgen früh wecken?
kur'-nen zee mikh *bi*-te *mor*gen froo veken

at 6 o'clock
um sechs Uhr
oom zekhs oor

at 6.30
um sechs Uhr dreißig
oom zekhs oor *dry*-sikh

at 7 o'clock
um sieben Uhr
oom *zee*ben oor

Can I have an outside line?
Kann ich bitte eine Amtsleitung haben?
kan ikh *bi*-te ine-e *amts*-lite-oong *hah*-ben

The ... doesn't work
Der/Die/Das ... funktioniert nicht
der/dee/das ... foonk-tsyoh-*neert* nikht

I need more coat hangers
Ich brauche noch mehr Kleiderbügel
ikh *brow*-khe nokh mayr *kly*der-boogel

Do you have a trouser press?
Haben Sie eine Hosenpresse für mich?
hah-ben zee ine-e *hoh*zen-pres-se foor mikh

■ **HOTEL** ■ **LAUNDRY** ■ **TELEPHONE**

| AUSVERKAUF | SALE / REDUCTIONS |
| LANGER DONNERSTAG | LATE NIGHT SHOPPING ON THURSDAYS |

How do I get to the main shopping area?
Wie komme ich zum Hauptgeschäftszentrum?
vee ko-me ikh tsoom howpt-geshefts-tsentroom

I'm looking for a present for...
Ich suche ein Geschenk für...
ikh zoo-khe ine geshenk foor...

my mother
meine Mutter
mine-e mooter

a child
ein Kind
ine kint

Where can I/we buy good...?
Wo kann man gut ... kaufen?
voh kan man goot ... kowfen

toys
Spielzeuge
shpeel-tsoyg-e

clothes
Kleidung
kly-doong

Can you recommend any good shops?
Können Sie ein paar gute Geschäfte empfehlen?
kur-nen zee ine pahr gute geshef-te emp-faylen

Which floor are shoes on?
Auf welchem Stockwerk sind die Schuhe?
owf vel-khem shtok-verk zint dee shoo-e

I'd like something similar to this
Ich möchte etwas Ähnliches wie dies
ikh mur'kh-te etvas ayn-li-khes vee dees

It's too expensive for me
Das ist mir zu teuer
das ist meer tsoo toy-er

Have you anything else?
Haben Sie noch etwas anderes?
hah-ben zee nokh etvas an-de-res

Is there a market?
Gibt es hier einen Markt?
gipt es heer ine-en markt

When?
Wann?
van

■ YOU MAY HEAR

Kann ich Ihnen helfen?
kan ikh ee-nen helfen
Can I help you?

Darf es sonst noch etwas sein?
darf es zonst nokh etvas zine
Would you like anything else?

■ CLOTHES ■ MEASUREMENTS & QUANTITIES

Most large shops in Germany are open all day approx. 0900-1800 Mon.-Fri. On Saturdays they are open until lunchtime, apart from the first Saturday of the month when they stay open all day.

baker's	BÄCKEREI	be-ke-**ry**
bookshop	BUCHHANDLUNG	**bookh**-hantloong
butcher's	FLEISCHEREI	fly-sher-**ry**
cake shop	KONDITOREI	kondi-toh-**ry**
clothes	KLEIDUNG	**kly**-doong
department store	WARENHAUS	**vah**ren-hows
dry-cleaner's	REINIGUNG	**ry**-nigoong
electrical goods	ELEKTROGESCHÄFT	e**lek**-tro-gesheft
fishmonger's	FISCHLADEN	**fish**-lahden
furniture	MÖBELGESCHÄFT	**mur'**bel-gesheft
gifts	GESCHENKARTIKEL	ge-**shenk**-arteekel
greengrocer's	GEMÜSELADEN	ge**moo**-ze-lahden
grocer's	LEBENSMITTELLADEN	**lay**bens-mittel-lahden
hairdresser's	FRISEUR	free-**zu'r**
health food shop	REFORMHAUS	**ray**form-hows
household (goods)	HAUSHALTSWAREN	**hows**-halts-vahren
ironmonger's	EISENWARENHANDLUNG	**ize**-en-vahren-hantloong
jeweller's	JUWELIER	yoovay-**leer**
market	MARKT	markt
pharmacy	APOTHEKE	apoh-**tay**-ke
records	SCHALLPLATTEN	**shal**-pla-ten
self-service	SELBSTBEDIENUNG	zelpst-be**dee**-noong
shoe shop	SCHUHGESCHÄFT	**shoo**-gesheft
shop	LADEN	**lah**-den
sports shop	SPORTGESCHÄFT	**sport**-gesheft
stationer's	SCHREIBWAREN-HANDLUNG	**shripe**-vahren-**hant**loong
supermarket	SUPERMARKT	**zooper**-markt
tobacconist's	TABAKLADEN	**tabak**-lahden
toy shop	SPIELWARENLADEN	**shpeel**-vahren-lahden

The local tourist office will have details of opening hours and the different excursions available in the area.

Where is the tourist office?
Wo ist die Touristeninformation?
*voh ist dee too**ris**-ten-infor-mat**syohn***

What can we visit in the area?
Was gibt es in der Gegend zu besichtigen?
*vas gipt es in der **gay**-gent tsoo be**zich**-tigen*

Have you any leaflets about it?
Haben Sie Broschüren davon?
hah**-ben zee bro-**shoo**ren da-**fon

When can we visit...?
Wann können wir ... besichtigen?
*van **kur'**-nen veer ... be**zikh**-tigen*

What day does it close?
An welchem Tag ist es zu?
*an **vel**-khem tahk ist es tsoo*

We'd like to go to...
Wir möchten nach...
veer mur'kh-ten nakh...

Are there any excursions?
Gibt es Ausflugsfahrten?
*gipt es **ows**-flooks-fahrten*

When does it leave?
Wann fährt er ab?
van fayrt er ap

Where does it leave from?
Wo fährt er ab?
voh fayrt er ap

How much does it cost to get in?
Was kostet der Eintritt?
*vas kostet der **ine**-trit*

Are there any reductions for...?
Gibt es Ermäßigung für...?
*gipt es er-**may**-sigoong foor...*

children	students	unemployed	senior citizens
Kinder	Studenten	Arbeitslose	Rentner
kinder	shtoo-**den**ten	**ar**-bites-loh-ze	rentner

■ ENTERTAINMENT ■ MAPS, GUIDES & NEWSPAPERS

AUFZUG
LIFT

AUSGANG
EXIT

AUSKUNFT
INFORMATION

AUSSER BETRIEB
OUT OF ORDER

AUSVERKAUF
SALE

BADEN VERBOTEN
NO BATHING

BELEGT
NO VACANCIES

BESETZT
ENGAGED

DAMEN
LADIES

DRÜCKEN
PUSH

EINGANG
ENTRANCE

EINTRITTSKARTEN
ENTRANCE TICKETS

ERDGESCHOSS
GROUND FLOOR

FAHRKARTEN HIER
ENTWERTEN
PUNCH TICKETS HERE

FAHRKARTEN-
SCHALTER
TICKET OFFICE

FREI
VACANT

FREMDENVERKEHRS-
BÜRO
TOURIST INFO.

GEÖFFNET
OPEN

GEPÄCKAUF-
BEWAHRUNG
LEFT LUGGAGE

GESCHLOSSEN
CLOSED

HEISS
HOT

HERREN
GENTS

IMBISSE
SNACKS

KALT
COLD

KASSE
CASH DESK

KEIN ZUTRITT
NO ENTRY

KLINGELN
RING

NICHTRAUCHER
NO SMOKING

NOTAUSGANG
EMERGENCY EXIT

RAUCHEN VERBOTEN
NO SMOKING

RAUCHER
SMOKING

RUHETAG
REST DAY (CLOSED)

SELBSTBEDIENUNG
SELF-SERVICE

TRINKWASSER
DRINKING WATER

UNTERGESCHOSS
BASEMENT

WEINPROBE
WINE TASTING

ZIEHEN
PULL

ZU DEN ZÜGEN
TO THE TRAINS

ZU MIETEN
FOR HIRE/TO RENT

ZU VERKAUFEN
FOR SALE

SKI PASS	DER SKIPASS
SKI INSTRUCTOR	DER SKILEHRER / DIE SKILEHRERIN
CROSS-COUNTRY SKIING	DER LANGLAUF

I want to hire skis
Ich möchte Skier leihen
*ikh mur'kh-te **shee**-er **ly**-en*

Are the boots / the poles included in the price?
Sind die Schuhe / die Stöcke im Preis inbegriffen?
*zint dee shoo-e / dee **shtur'**-khe im price **in**-be-griffen*

Can you adjust my bindings, please?
Könnten Sie bitte meine Bindungen einstellen?
*kur'n-ten zee **bi**-te mine-e **bin**-doongen **ine**-shtellen*

How much is a pass for...?   a day   a week
Was kostet ein Paß für...?
vas kostet ine pas foor...

einen Tag
ine-en tahk

eine Woche
*ine-e **vo**-khe*

Do you have a map of the ski runs?
Haben Sie eine Pistenkarte?
***hah**-ben zee ine-e **pis**ten-kar-te*

When is the last chair-lift?
Wann ist der letzte Skilift?
*van ist der **let**-ste skilift*

■ YOU MAY HEAR

Welche Länge brauchen Sie?
***vel**-khe leng-e **brow**-khen zee*
What length skis do you want?

Welche Schuhgröße haben Sie?
***vel**-khe **shoo**-grur'-se **hah**-ben zee*
What is your shoe size?

Es besteht Lawinengefahr
*es be**shtayt** la**vee**-nen-gefahr*
There is danger of avalanches

Diese Piste ist gesperrt
*dee-ze pis-te ist ge**shpert***
This run is closed off

MATCH / GAME	DER WETTKAMPF / DAS SPIEL
TENNIS COURT	DER TENNISPLATZ
GOLF COURSE	DER GOLFPLATZ

Where can we...?
Wo können wir...?
*voh **kur'**-nen veer ...*

play tennis
Tennis spielen
tennis shpeelen

play golf
Golf spielen
golf shpeelen

go swimming
schwimmen
***shvim**men*

go jogging
joggen
joggen

How much is it per hour?
Was kostet es pro Stunde?
vas kostet es proh shtoon-de

Can we hire rackets/clubs? *(same word)*
Kann man Schläger leihen?
*kan man **shlay**-ger **ly**-en*

We'd like to go to see *(name team)* **play**
Wir möchten ein Spiel mit ... sehen
*veer mur'kh-ten ine shpeel mit ... **zay**-en*

Where can I/we get tickets?
Wo gibt es Karten?
voh gipt es karten

How do I/we get to the stadium?
Wie kommt man zum Stadion?
*vee komt man tsoom **shta**-dyohn*

Which is your favourite team? *(familiar)*
Was ist deine Lieblingsmannschaft?
*vas ist dine-e **leep**lings-**man**shaft*

Would you like a game of tennis?
Möchten Sie Tennis spielen?
mur'kh-ten zee tennis shpeelen

■ **LEISURE/INTERESTS** ■ **SKIING** ■ **WALKING**

*All these items can be bought at **die Schreibwarenhandlung.***

biro	der Kuli	**koo**lee
cardboard	der Karton	karton
cards (greetings)	die Grußkarten	**groos**-karten
crayons (wax)	die Wachsmalstifte	**vaks**-mahl-shtif-te
envelopes	die Umschläge	**oom**shlay-ge
exercise book	das Heft	heft
felt-tip pen	der Filzstift	**filts**-shtift
folder	der Aktendeckel	**akten**-dekel
glue	das Uhu®	**oo**-hoo
ink	die Tinte	**tin**-te
ink cartridge	die Patrone	pa**troh**-ne
magazine	die Zeitschrift	**tsite**-shrift
newspaper	die Zeitung	**tsy**-toong
note pad	der Notizblock	no**teets**-blok
paints	die Farben	farben
paper	das Papier	pa**peer**
paper (recycled)	das Umweltpapier	**oom**velt-pa**peer**
paperclip	die Büroklammer	boo**roh**-klammer
pen (fountain)	der Füller	fooler
pencil	der Bleistift	**bly**-shtift
pencil sharpener	der Bleistiftspitzer	**bly**-shtift-shpitser
postcard	die Ansichtskarte	**an**zikhts-kar-te
rubber	der Radiergummi	ra**deer**-goomee
ruler	das Lineal	leenee-**al**
Sellotape®	der Tesafilm®	**tayza**-film
stapler	die Heftmaschine	**heft**-ma**shee**-ne
staples	die Heftklammern	**heft**-klammern
writing paper	das Briefpapier	**breef**-pa**peer**

■ OFFICE ■ SHOPPING

*In Germany it is practically impossible to flag down a taxi in the street. You have to find a taxi rank, **Taxistand**, or phone for one. You can often find adverts for taxi firms in public telephones and you must give your name and the address of the phone box which will be written under the word **Standort***

I want a taxi
Ich hätte gern ein Taxi
ikh het-te gern ine taxi

Where can I get a taxi?
Wo bekomme ich hier ein Taxi?
*voh be-**ko**-me ikh heer ine taxi*

Please order me a taxi
Bitte bestellen Sie mir ein Taxi
***bi**-te be-**shte**llen zee meer ine taxi*

straightaway
sofort
*zo-**fort***

for *(time)*
für ... Uhr
foor...oor

My name is...
Ich heiße...
*ikh **hy**-se...*

The address is...
Die Adresse ist...
*dee a-**dre**-se ist...*

How much is it...?
Was kostet die Fahrt ...?
vas kostet dee fahrt...

to the centre
ins Zentrum
*ins **tsen**troom*

to the station
zum Bahnhof
*tsoom **bahn**-hof*

to the airport
zum Flughafen
*tsoom **flook**-hafen*

to this address
zu dieser Adresse
*tsoo deezer a-**dre**-se*

How much is it?
Was kostet das?
vas kostet das

Why is it so much?
Warum ist das so teuer?
*vah**room** ist das zoh **toy**-er*

I'm afraid I've nothing smaller
Ich habe es leider nicht kleiner
*ikh **hah**-be es **ly**-der nikht kline-er*

I need a receipt
Ich brauche eine Quittung
*ikh **brow**-khe ine-e **kvi**-toong*

I'm in a hurry
Ich habe es sehr eilig
*ikh **hah**-be es zayr **eye**-likh*

Is it far?
Ist es weit?
ist es vite

I have to catch the ... o'clock flight to...
Ich muß zum Flug um ... Uhr nach...
ikh moos tsoom flook oom ... oor nakh...

■ BUS ■ METRO ■ TELEPHONE

To phone Germany from the UK, the international codes are
010 49 *(for what was West Germany), and* **010 37** *(for what was East Germany), then the area code (e.g. Bonn-**228**, Leipzig-**41**) followed by the number you require. (Other international codes: Austria* **010 43***, Switzerland* **010 41***). To phone the UK from Germany, Austria and Switzerland dial* **00 44***, plus the UK area code without the first 0, e.g., London (0)**71** or (0)**81**.*

PHONECARD	**DIE TELEFONKARTE**
TELEPHONE DIRECTORY	**DAS TELEFONBUCH**
YELLOW PAGES	**DIE GELBEN SEITEN**
COLLECT / REVERSE CHARGE CALL	**DAS R-GESPRÄCH**
PAYPHONE	**DER MÜNZFERNSPRECHER**
TO DIAL DIRECT	**DURCHWÄHLEN**

I want to make a phone call
Ich möchte telefonieren
*ikh mur'kh-te taylay-fo-**nee**ren*

What coins do I need?
Was für Münzen brauche ich?
*vas foor **moon**-tsen **brow**-khe ikh*

Can you show me how this phone works?
Können Sie mir zeigen, wie dieses Telefon funktioniert?
kur'**-nen zee meer **tsy**-gen vee dee-zes taylay-**fohn** foonk-tsyoh-**neert

Where can I buy a phonecard?
Wo kann ich eine Telefonkarte kaufen?
*voh kan ikh ine-e taylay**fon**-kar-te kowfen*

Herr Braun, please
Herr Braun, bitte
*hayr brown **bi**-te*

Extension ..., please
Apparat ..., bitte
*apa-**raht** ... **bi**-te*

Can I speak to Mr.../Mrs...?
Kann ich mit Herrn.../Frau... sprechen?
*kan ikh mit haym.../frow... **shpre**-khen*

This is Jim Brown
Hier ist Jim Brown
heer ist jim brown

An outside line, please
Eine Amtsleitung, bitte
ine-e amts-ly-toong bi-te

I can't get through
Ich komme nicht durch
ikh ko-me nikht doorkh

We were cut off
Wir sind unterbrochen worden
veer zint oonter-bro-khen vorden

It's constantly engaged
Da ist immer besetzt
da ist immer bezetst

■ YOU MAY HEAR

Hallo
halo
Hello

Wer spricht, bitte?
ver shprikht bi-te
Who is calling?

Augenblick, ich verbinde
owgen-blik ikh ferbin-de
Just a moment, I'm trying to connect you

Es ist besetzt
es ist bezetst
It's engaged

Bitte rufen Sie später wieder an
bi-te roofen zee shpayter veeder an
Please try again later

Soll ich etwas ausrichten?
zoll ikh etvas ows-rikhten
Can I take a message?

Sie haben sich verwählt
zee hah-ben zikh fervaylt
You've got a wrong number

Hier spricht der automatische Anrufbeantworter von...
heer shprikht der owto-mah-tish-e an-roof-bayant-worter fon...
This is the answering machine of...

Bitte sprechen Sie nach dem Signalton
bi-te shpre-khen zee nakh dem zig-nahl-ton
Please leave a message after the tone

■ BUSINESS–MEETING ■ FAX ■ OFFICE

REMOTE CONTROL	DIE FERNBEDIENUNG
SOAP	DIE SEIFENOPER
VIDEO RECORDER	DER VIDEORECORDER
NEWS	DIE NACHRICHTEN
TO SWITCH ON	EINSCHALTEN
TO SWITCH OFF	AUSSCHALTEN
CARTOONS	DER TRICKFILM

Where is the television?
Wo ist der Fernseher?
*voh ist der **fern**-zayer*

How do you switch it on?
Wie geht er an?
vee gayt er an

Which button do I press?
Welchen Knopf muß ich drücken?
***vel**-khen k-nopf moos ikh **droo**-ken*

Please could you lower the volume?
Könnten Sie bitte leiser stellen?
***kur'n**-ten zee **bi**-te **ly**-zer shtellen*

May I turn the volume up?
Darf ich lauter stellen?
*darf ikh **low**-ter shtellen*

What's on television?
Was gibt es im Fernsehen?
*vas gipt es im **fern**-zayen*

When is the news?
Wann kommen Nachrichten?
*van kommen **nakh**-rikhten*

Do you have any English-speaking programmes?
Haben Sie Programme auf Englisch?
***hah**-ben zee pro**gram**-me owf **eng**-lish*

When are the children's programmes?
Wann sind die Kinderprogramme?
*van zint dee **kin**der-pro**gram**-me*

Have you...?	**any English videos**	**a satellite dish**
Haben Sie...?	englische Videos	eine Satellitenschüssel
***hah**-ben zee...*	***eng**-lish-e **vee**-day-os*	*ine-e zatel-**lee**ten-shoosel*

82

Very often in German theatres you have to leave your coat in a particular place, determined by your seat number, and your ticket is also your cloakroom ticket.

CLOAKROOM	DIE GARDEROBE
PLAY	DAS THEATERSTÜCK
SEAT	DER PLATZ

What's on at the theatre?
Was gibt es im Theater?
vas gipt es im tay-ahter

How do I/we get there?
Wie kommt man hin?
vee komt man hin

How much are the tickets?
Was kosten die Karten?
vas kosten dee kar-ten

I'd like two tickets...
Ich hätte gern zwei Karten...
ikh het-te gern tsvy kar-ten...

for tonight
für heute abend
foor hoy-te ahbent

for tomorrow night
für morgen abend
foor morgen ahbent

for 5th August
für den fünften August
foor den foonf-ten owgoost

in the stalls
im Parkett
im par-kett

in the circle
im ersten Rang
im ers-ten rang

in the upper circle
im zweiten Rang
im tsvy-ten rang

How long is the interval?
Wie lang ist die Pause?
vee lang ist dee pow-ze

Is there a bar?
Gibt es eine Bar?
gipt es ine-e bar

When does the performance end?
Wann ist die Vorstellung zu Ende?
van ist dee for-shtelloong tsoo en-de

I enjoyed that
Es hat mir gut gefallen
es hat meer goot gefal-en

It was very good
Es war sehr gut
es vahr zayr goot

■ ENTERTAINMENT ■ LEISURE/INTERESTS

> The 24-hour clock is used a lot more in continental Europe than in Britain. After 1200 midday, it continues: **1300**-*dreizehn Uhr*, **1400**-*vierzehn Uhr*, **1500**-*fünfzehn Uhr*, etc. until **2400**-*vierundzwanzig Uhr*. With the 24-hour clock, the words *Viertel* (quarter) and *Halb* (half) aren't used:
>
> **13.15** (1.15pm)   *dreizehn Uhr fünfzehn*
> **19.30** (7.30pm)   *neunzehn Uhr dreißig*
> **22.45** (10.45pm) *zweiundzwanzig Uhr fünfundvierzig*

What time is it, please?	**am**	**pm**
Wie spät ist es, bitte?	morgens	abends
vee shpayt ist es **bi**-te	**mor**gens	**ah**-bents

It's ...	**2 o'clock**	**3 o'clock**	**6 o'clock** (etc.)
Es ist...	zwei Uhr	drei Uhr	sechs Uhr
es ist...	tsvy oor	dry oor	zekhs oor

It's half past 8	**at midnight**
Es ist halb neun (in German you say half to 9)	um Mitternacht
es ist halp noyn	oom **mitter**-nakht

9	neun Uhr
	noyn oor
9.10	neun Uhr zehn
	noyn oor tsayn
quarter past 9	Viertel nach neun (Austria: *viertel zehn*)
	feertel nakh noyn
9.20	neun Uhr zwanzig
	*noyn oor **tsvan**-tsikh*
half past 9 / 9.30	halb zehn / neun Uhr dreißig
	*halp tsayn / noyn oor **dry**-sikh*
9.35	neun Uhr fünfunddreißig
	*noyn oor foonf-oont-**dry**-sich*
quarter to 10	Viertel vor zehn (Austria: *dreiviertel zehn*)
	feertel for tsayn
10 to 10	zehn vor zehn
	tsayn for tsayn

■ **NUMBERS**

When do you open?
Wann öffnen Sie?
*van **ur'f**-nen zee*

When do you close?
Wann schließen Sie?
*van **shlee**-sen zee*

at 3 o'clock
um drei Uhr
oom dry oor

before 3 o'clock
vor drei Uhr
for dry oor

after 3 o'clock
nach drei Uhr
nakh dry oor

today
heute
hoy-te

tonight
heute abend
hoy-te ahbent

tomorrow
morgen
morgen

yesterday
gestern
gestern

the day before yesterday
vorgestern
for-gestern

the day after tomorrow
übermorgen
oober-morgen

in the morning
morgens
morgens

this morning
heute morgen
hoy-te morgen

in the afternoon
am Nachmittag
am nakh-mi-tahk

in the evening
am Abend
am ahbent

at half past 7
um halb acht
oom halp akht

at about 10 o'clock
etwa um zehn Uhr
etva oom tsayn oor

in an hour's time
in einer Stunde
in ine-er shtoon-de

in a while
bald
balt

two hours ago
vor zwei Stunden
for tsvy shtoonden

soon
bald
balt

early
früh
froo

late
spät
shpayt

later
später
shpayter

I'll do it...
Ich mache es...
ikh ma-khe es...

as soon as possible
so bald wie möglich
zo balt vee mur'k-likh

...at the latest
...spätestens
...shpay-testens

85

*Be sure to check if there is a supplement, **ein Zuschlag**, to pay before you board the train. It costs less if you buy it with your ticket. The ticket and information office for the German railways are marked **Reisezentrum***

ICE *(InterCity Express)*	special fare applies
EC / IC *(EuroCity / InterCity)*	supplement payable
IR *(Inter Regio)*	fast regional trains
RSB *(Regional Schnell Bahn)*	suburban rail network

When is the next train to....?
Wann geht der nächste Zug nach...?
*van gayt der **nekh**-ste tzook nakh...*

Two return tickets to...
Zwei Rückfahrkarten nach...
*tsvy **rook**far-karten nakh...*

A single to...
Einmal einfach nach...
__ine__-mal __ine__-fakh nakh...

Ist / 2nd class
Erster / Zweiter Klasse
__er__-ster / __tsvy__-ter __kla__-se

Smoking / Non smoking
Raucher / Nichtraucher
__row__-kher / __nicht__-row-kher

Is there a supplement to pay?
Muß ich einen Zuschlag zahlen?
moos ikh ine-en __tsoo__shlak __tsah__-len

I want to book a seat on the ICE to Bonn
Ich möchte einen Platz im ICE nach Bonn buchen
ikh mur'kh-te ine-en plats im ee-tsay-ay nakh bon __boo__-khen

When is the first / last train to...?
Wann geht der erste / der letzte Zug nach...?
van gayt der __er__-ste / der lets-te tsook nakh...

When does it arrive in...?
Wann kommt er in ... an?
van komt er in ... an

Do I need to change?
Muß ich umsteigen?
moos ikh __oom__-shty-gen

Where?
Wo?
voh

How long is there for the connection?
Wieviel Zeit habe ich zum nächsten Zug?
*vee**feel** tsite **hah**-be ikh tsoom **nekh**-sten tsook*

Will my connecting train wait?
Wartet der Anschlußzug?
***var**-tet der **an**-shloos-tsook*

Which platform does it leave from?
Von welchem Bahnsteig fährt er ab?
*fon **vel**-khem **bahn**-shtike fayrt er ap*

Does the train to... leave from here?
Fährt hier der Zug nach ... ab?
fayrt heer der tsook nakh ... ap

Is this the train for...?
Ist das der Zug nach...?
ist das der tsook nakh...

When will it leave?
Wann fährt er ab?
van fayrt er ap

Why is the train delayed?
Warum hat der Zug Verspätung?
*vah**room** hat der tsook fer-**shpay**-toong*

Does the train stop at...?
Hält der Zug in...?
helt der tsook in...

Please let me know when we get to...
Bitte sagen Sie mir, wenn wir in ... ankommen
***bi**-te **zah**gen zee mir ven veer in ... **an**-kommen*

Is there a buffet on the train?
Hat der Zug einen Speisewagen?
*hat der tsook ine-en **shpy**-ze-vahgen*

Is this free? *(seat)*
Ist hier noch frei?
ist heer nokh fry

Excuse me
Entschuldigung
*ent**shool**-digoong*

Although vegetarianism is gradually becoming more popular, few restaurants offer vegetarian options.

Are there any vegetarian restaurants here?
Gibt es hier vegetarische Restaurants?
*gipt es heer vaygay-**ta**rish-e restoh-**rongs***

Do you have any vegetarian dishes?
Haben Sie vegetarische Gerichte?
***hah**-ben zee vaygay-**ta**rish-e ge-**rikh**-te*

Which dishes have no meat / fish?
Welche Gerichte sind ohne Fleisch / Fisch?
***vel**-khe ge-**rikh**-te zint **oh**-ne flysh / fish*

What fish dishes do you have?
Was für Fischgerichte haben Sie?
*vas foor **fish**-gerikh-te **hah**-ben zee*

I'd like pasta as a main course
Ich möchte als Hauptgericht Nudeln
*ikh mur'kh-te als **howpt**-gerikht **noo**deln*

I don't eat meat
Ich esse kein Fleisch
*ikh **es**-se kine flysh*

What do you recommend?
Was können Sie empfehlen?
*vas **kur'**-nen zee emp-**fay**len*

Is it made with vegetable stock?
Ist das mit Gemüsebrühe gemacht?
*ist das mit ge**moo**-ze-broo-he ge-**makht***

■ POSSIBLE DISHES

Gemüsestrudel *vegetable-filled strudel*
Kartoffelpuffer *potato pancakes*
Käseplatte *selection of cheeses*
Omelette mit Champignons *mushroom omelette*
Pfifferling mit Semmelklops *chanterelle mushrooms with dumpling and sauce*
Topfenstrudel *strudel filled with soft cheese*

■ EATING OUT

Are there any guided walks?
Gibt es geführte Wanderungen?
*gipt es ge-**foor**-te **van**-de-roongen*

Do you have details?
Haben Sie Informationen dazu?
hah**-ben zee infor-mat**syoh**-nen dat**soo

Is there a guide to local walks?
Gibt es einen Wanderführer von dieser Gegend?
*gipt es ine-en vander-**foo**rer fon deezer **gay**gent*

How many kilometres is the walk?
Wie lang ist die Wanderung?
*vee lang ist dee **van**-deroong*

Is it very steep?
Ist sie sehr steil?
ist zee zayr shtyl

How long will the walk take?
Wie lange werden wir für die Wanderung brauchen?
*vee lang-e verden veer foor dee **van**-deroong **brow**-khen*

We'd like to go climbing
Wir möchten klettern gehen
*veer mur'kh-ten **klet**tern gayen*

Do I/we need walking boots?
Braucht man Wanderstiefel?
*browkht man **van**der-shteefel*

Should we take...?	**water**	**food**	**waterproofs**
Müssen wir ... mitnehmen?	Essen	Wasser	Regenzeug
***moo**sen veer ... **mit**-naymen*	essen	vasser	**ray**gen-tsoyk

What time does it get dark?
Wann wird es dunkel?
van virt es doonkel

■ MAPS, GUIDES... ■ SIGHTSEEING & TOURIST OFFICE

What is the weather forecast?
Wie ist der Wetterbericht?
*vee ist der **vet**ter-berikht*

It's sunny	It's raining	It's snowing	It's windy
Es ist sonnig	Es regnet	Es schneit	Es ist windig
*es ist **zon**nikh*	*es **rayg**net*	*es shnite*	*es ist **vin**-dikh*

What a lovely day!
Was für ein herrlicher Tag!
*vas foor ine **her**-likh-er tahk*

What awful weather!
Was für Mistwetter!
*vas foor **mist**-vetter*

What will the weather be like tomorrow?
Wie wird das Wetter morgen?
*vee virt das vetter **mor**gen*

Do you think it will rain?
Glauben Sie, es gibt Regen?
***glow**ben zee es gipt raygen*

Do I need an umbrella?
Brauche ich einen Schirm?
***brow**-khe ikh ine-en shirm*

When will it stop raining?
Wann hört der Regen wohl auf?
van hur't der raygen vohl owf

It's very hot
Es ist sehr heiß
es ist zayr hice

Do you think there will be a storm?
Glauben Sie, es gibt Sturm?
***glow**ben zee es gipt shtoorm*

Do you think it will snow?
Glauben Sie, es gibt Schnee?
***glow**ben zee es gipt shnay*

What is the temperature?
Wie ist die Temperatur?
*vee ist dee tempe-ra**toor***

■ **MAKING FRIENDS**

The wine list, please
Die Weinkarte, bitte
*dee **vine**kar-te **bi**-te*

Can you recommend a good wine?
Können Sie mir einen guten Wein empfehlen?
*kur'-nen zee meer ine-en **goo**-ten vine emp-**fay**len*

A bottle of house wine
Eine Flasche Hauswein
*ine-e **fla**-she **hows**vine*

A glass of white wine / red wine
Ein Glas Weißwein / Rotwein
*ine glahs **vice**vine / **roht**vine*

A bottle of red wine
Eine Flasche Rotwein
*ine-e **fla**-she **roht**vine*

A bottle of white wine
Eine Flasche Weißwein
*ine-e **fla**-she **vice**vine*

Wines are usually categorized according to three criteria: the overall growing area, the village or even vineyard where they are produced, and the type of grape they are made from. Major grape varieties include **Riesling Edelzwicker Gewürztraminer** *and* **Müller-Thurgau**

Important wine-growing areas in Germany and Austria include:

Ahr *small valley north of the Moselle, producing mainly pleasant, light red wines*

Baden *the region around Freiburg in the Upper Rhine valley, producing pleasant, light, mainly white and rosé wines*

Burgenland *region in Austria producing mainly sweet wines*

Franken *important wine-growing area in Northern Bavaria, producing dry, full-bodied wines*

Mosel-Saar-Ruwer *region along the rivers Moselle, Saar and Ruwer, producing white wines, many of them dry*

Rheinpfalz *Palatinate region, producing mainly white wines*

Rheinhessen *quality wine region along the banks of the Rhine*

Wachau *major wine-growing area in Austria, just west of Vienna*

Württemberg *small wine growing area in southern Germany*

The names of the villages and vineyards producing wines are innumerable. The name of the wine is often the name of the village (e.g. Nierstein) plus the name of the particular vineyard (e.g. Gutes Domtal) which combined become **Niersteiner Gutes Domtal**

CONT...

Amongst the most well-known names are:

Bereich Bernkastel *on the river Moselle, producing crisp whites*

Erbach *area near Eltville in the Rheingau/Palatinate region, producing scented white wines mainly from the Riesling grape*

Gumpoldkirchen *spicy white wine from Austria*

Hochheim *strong white wines the from the Rheingau region*

Kaiserstuhl *region near Freiburg, produing light white and rosé wines which are best drunk young*

Nierstein *village in the Rheingau region, producing medium to sweet white Rheinwein (e.g.* **Niersteiner Gutes Domtal)**

Oppenheim *village on the Rhine, producing fine white wines*

Volkach *town in Franken, producing fine, rather dry white wines*

Other words to look out for are:

Eiswein *a rich, naturally sweet, white wine made from grapes which are harvested only after a period of frost*

halbtrocken *medium-dry*

Landwein *similar to French 'vin de pays'*

Prädikatswein *highest category of quality wines*

QbA *quality wine from a specified region*

Tafelwein *lowest quality wine, similar to French 'vin de table'*

trocken *dry*

■ OTHER DRINKS

What liqueurs do you have?
Was für Liköre haben Sie?
*vas foor lee-**kur**'-re **hah**-ben zee*

Apfelkorn *apple brandy*

Danziger Goldwasser *brandy with tiny bits of gold leaf*

Himbeergeist *raspberry brandy which is very strong and clear*

Kirschwasser *cherry brandy*

Schnaps *brandy*

Slivovitz *plum brandy (Austria)*

■ DRINKING ■ EATING OUT

What work do you do?
Was machen Sie beruflich?
*vas **ma**khen zee be-**roo**flikh*

Do you enjoy it?
Macht es Ihnen Spaß?
makht es ee-nen shpahs

I'm...
Ich bin...
ikh bin...

a teacher
Lehrer(in)
***lay**-rer(in)*

a manager
Manager(in)
***man**ager(in)*

a postman
Briefträger(in)
***breef**-treger(in)*

I work in...
Ich arbeite in...
*ikh **ar**-by-te in...*

a shop
einem Geschäft
*ine-em ge**sheft***

a factory
einer Fabrik
*ine-er fa**breek***

a bank
einer Bank
ine-er bank

I work from home
Ich arbeite zu Hause
*ikh **ar**-by-te tsoo **how**-ze*

I'm self-employed
Ich bin selbständig
*ikh bin **selp**-shtendikh*

I am unemployed
Ich bin arbeitslos
*ikh bin **ar**-bites-los*

It's very difficult to get a job at the moment
Es ist im Augenblick sehr schwer, Arbeit zu finden
*es ist im **ow**gen-blikh zayr shvayr **ar**-bite tsoo finden*

What hours do you work?
Wieviele Stunden arbeiten Sie?
*vee**fee**-le shtoon-den **ar**-bite-en zee*

full-time
ganztags
***gants**-tahks*

part-time
halbtags
***halp**-tahks*

I work from 9 to 5
Ich arbeite von neun bis fünf
*ikh **ar**-by-te fon noyn bis foonf*

from Monday to Friday
Montag bis Freitag
***mohn**tahk bis **fry**-tahk*

How much holiday do you get?
Wieviel Urlaub haben Sie?
*vee**feel oor**lowp **hah**-ben zee*

What do you want to be when you grow up?
Was möchtest du einmal werden, wenn du groß bist?
*vas mur'kh-test doo **ine**-mal **ver**den ven doo grohs bist*

■ **MAKING FRIENDS**

NOUNS

In German all nouns begin with a capital letter. The plural forms vary from noun to noun – there is no universal plural as in English (cat – cats, dog – dogs):

singular	plural
Mann	**Männer**
Frau	**Frauen**
Tisch	**Tische**

(In the dictionary, plural forms appear where they may be useful.)

German nouns are *masculine* (m), *feminine* (f) or *neuter* (nt), and this is shown by the words for **the** and **a(n)** used before them:

	masculine	feminine	neuter
the	der Mann	die Frau	das Licht
a, an	ein Mann	eine Frau	ein Licht

The plural for **the** for all forms is **die**:

die Männer	**die Frauen**	**die Lichte**

There is no plural for the **ein** form. The plural noun is used on its own.

From the phrases in this book you will see that the endings for the word for **the** vary according to what part the noun plays in the sentence:

If the noun is the subject of the sentence, i.e. carrying out the action, then it is in the *nominative* case (the one found in dictionaries), e.g. **der Mann steht auf (the man stands up)**. The subject **der Mann** comes before the verb.

If the noun is the direct object of the sentence, i.e. the action of the verb is being carried on the noun, then the noun is in the *accusative* case, e.g. **ich sehe den Mann (I see the man)**. Note how the ending of **der** has changed to **den**. The same applies to **ein**, e.g. **ich sehe einen Mann (I see a man)**.

If you see in front of the English noun – **of**, **'s**, or **s'** – then the noun is in the *genitive* case (i.e. it belongs to someone or something), e.g. **das Haus der Frau (the woman's house)**. Note how the ending of **die** (Frau) has changed to **der**. The same applies to **ein**, e.g. **das Haus einer Frau (a woman's house)**.

If you see **to the** or **to a** in front of the English noun, then the noun is in the *dative* case, e.g. **ich gebe es der Frau (I give it to the woman)**. Note how the ending of **die** (Frau) has changed to **der**. The same applies to **ein**, e.g. **ich gebe es einer Frau (I give it to a woman)**.

Several other words used before nouns have similar endings to **der** and **ein**.
Those like **der** are:
dieser this ; jener that ; jeder each ; welcher which
Those like **ein** are:
mein my ; dein your (familiar sing.) ; **Ihr your** (polite sing. and plural) ; **sein his ; ihr her ; unser our ; euer your** (familiar plural); **ihr their**

Here are the cases for **der**:

	masculine	feminine	neuter	plural
Nominative	der Mann	die Frau	das Licht	die Frauen
Accusative	den Mann	die Frau	das Licht	die Frauen
Genitive	des Mannes	der Frau	des Lichtes	der Frauen
Dative	dem Mann	der Frau	dem Licht	den Frauen

Here are the cases for **ein**:

	masculine	feminine	neuter
Nominative	ein Mann	eine Frau	ein Licht
Accusative	einen Mann	eine Frau	ein Licht
Genitive	eines Mannes	einer Frau	eines Lichtes
Dative	einem Mann	einer Frau	einem Licht

The word **kein (no, not any)** also has the same endings as for **ein**, except that it can be used in the plural:

Nominative	keine Männer
Accusative	keine Männer
Genitive	keiner Männer
Dative	keinen Männern

ADJECTIVES

When adjectives are used before a noun, their endings vary like the words for **der** and **ein**, depending on the gender (*masculine, feminine* or *neuter*) and whether the noun is plural, and how the noun is used in the sentence (whether it is the subject, object, etc.). Here are examples using the adjective **klug – clever**

	masculine	feminine
Nominative	**der kluge Mann** **ein kluger Mann**	**die kluge Frau** **eine kluge Frau**
Accusative	**den klugen Mann** **einen klugen Mann**	**die kluge Frau** **eine kluge Frau**
Genitive	**des klugen Mannes** **eines klugen Mannes**	**der klugen Frau** **einer klugen Frau**
Dative	**dem klugen Mann** **einem klugen Mann**	**der klugen Frau** **einer klugen Frau**

	neuter	plural
Nominative	**das kluge Kind** **ein kluges Kind**	**die klugen Männer** **kluge Frauen**
Accusative	**das kluge Kind** **ein kluges Kind**	**die klugen Männer** **kluge Frauen**
Genitive	**des klugen Kindes** **eines klugen Kindes**	**der klugen Männer** **kluger Frauen**
Dative	**dem klugen Kind** **einem klugen Kind**	**den klugen Männern** **klugen Frauen**

When the adjective follows the verb, then there is no agreement:

der Mann ist klug
die Frau ist klug
das Kind ist klug

MY, YOUR, HIS, HER

These words all take the same endings as for **ein** and they agree
with the noun they accompany, i.e. whether *masculine*,
feminine, *neuter*, *plural* and according to the function of the
noun (*nominative*, *accusative*, etc.):

mein Mann kommt my husband is coming *(nom.)*
ich liebe meinen Mann I love my husband *(acc.)*
das Auto meines Mannes My husband's car *(gen.)*
ich gebe es meinem Mann I give it to my husband *(dat.)*
meine Kinder kommen my children are coming *(nom. pl.)*
ich liebe meine Kinder I love my children *(acc. pl.)*
die Spielsachen meiner Kinder my children's toys *(gen. pl.)*
ich gebe es meinen Kindern I give it to my children *(dat. pl.)*

Other words which take these endings are:
dein your *(familiar sing.)* ; **sein** his ; **ihr** her ; **unser** our ; **euer**
your *(familiar plural)* ; **ihr** your *(polite sing. and plural)* ; **ihr** their

PRONOUNS

subject		*direct object*	
I	ich	**me**	mich
you *(familiar sing.)*	du	**you** *(familiar sing.)*	dich
he/it	er	**him/it**	ihn
she/it	sie	**her/it**	sie
it *(neuter)*	es	**it** *(neuter)*	es
we	wir	**us**	uns
you *(familiar plural)*	ihr	**you** *(familiar plural)*	euch
you *(polite sing. & pl.)*	Sie	**you** *(polite sing. & pl.)*	Sie
they *(all genders)*	sie	**them** *(all genders)*	sie

Indirect object pronouns are:

to me mir ; **to you** *(familiar sing.)* dir ; **to him/it** ihm ; **to her/it**
ihr ; **to it** *(neuter)* ihm ; **to us** uns ; **to you** *(familiar plural)* euch ;
to you *(polite sing. and plural)* Ihnen ; **to them** ihnen

YOU

There are two ways of addressing people in German: the familiar form – **du** (when talking to just one person you know well), **ihr** (when talking to more than one person you know well), and the polite form – **Sie** (always written with a capital letter), which can be used for one or more people.

VERBS

There are two main types of verb in German – **weak** verbs (which are regular) and **strong** verbs (which are irregular).

	weak SPIELEN **to play**	strong HELFEN **to help**
ich	spiele	helfe
du	spielst	hilfst
er/sie/es	spielt	hilft
wir	spielen	helfen
ihr	spielt	hilft
Sie	spielen	helfen
sie	spielen	helfen

Other examples of **strong** verbs are:

	SEIN **to be**	HABEN **to have**
ich	bin	habe
du	bist	hast
er/sie/es	ist	hat
wir	sind	haben
ihr	seid	habt
Sie	sind	haben
sie	sind	haben

To make a verb negative, add **nicht**:

ich verstehe nicht	**I don't understand**
das funktioniert nicht	**it doesn't work**

PAST TENSE

Here are a number of useful past tenses:

ich war	I was
wir waren	we were
Sie waren	you were *(polite)*
ich hatte	I had
wir hatten	we had
Sie hatten	you had *(polite)*
ich/er/sie/es spielte	I/he/she/it played
Sie/wir/sie spielten	you/we/they played
ich/er/sie/es half	I/he/she/it helped
Sie/wir/sie halfen	you/we/they helped

Another past form corresponds to the English **have ...ed** and uses the verb **haben to have**:

ich habe gespielt	I have played
wir haben geholfen	we have helped

In German the present tense is very often used where we would use the future tense in English:

ich schicke ein Fax	I will send a fax
ich schreibe einen Brief	I will write a letter

a *(with 'der' words)*	ein
(with 'die' words)	eine
(with 'das' words)	ein
abbey	die Abtei
about *(concerning)*	über
(place)	umher ; herum
(approximately)	ungefähr
about 4 o'clock	ungefähr 4 Uhr
above *(overhead)*	oben
(higher than)	über
accident	der Unfall
accommodation	die Unterkunft
ache	weh tun
my head aches	mir tut der Kopf weh
adaptor *(electrical)*	der Zwischenstecker
address	die Adresse
adhesive tape	das Klebeband
admission charge	der Eintrittspreis
adult *m/f*	der/die Erwachsene
advance: *in advance*	im voraus
advertisement	die Anzeige
after *(afterwards)*	danach
(place, order)	hinter
afternoon	der Nachmittag
aftershave	das Rasierwasser
again	wieder
agent *m/f*	der/die Vertreter(in)
(organization)	die Vertretung
ago: *long ago*	vor langer Zeit
a week ago	vor einer Woche
agree	vereinbaren
AIDS	das AIDS
air-conditioning	die Klimaanlage
airline	die Fluggesellschaft
air mail: *by air mail*	per Luftpost

English	German
air-mattress	die Luftmatratze
airport	der Flughafen
aisle *(in theatre)*	der Gang
(in church)	das Seitenschiff
alarm call	der Weckruf
alarm clock	der Wecker
alcoholic	alkoholisch
all	alle
allergic to	allergisch gegen
allow	erlauben
allowance *(customs)*	die zollfreie Menge
all right *(agreed)*	in Ordnung
are you all right?	*geht es Ihnen gut?*
almond	die Mandel
almost	fast
also	auch
always	immer
am	see **(to be)** GRAMMAR
ambulance	der Krankenwagen
America	Amerika
American	amerikanisch
(person) m/f	der/die Amerikaner(in)
anaesthetic	die Narkose
and	und
angry	zornig
another *(additional)*	noch ein(e/s)
(different)	ein anderer
answer n	die Antwort
answer vb	antworten
antibiotic	das Antibiotikum
antifreeze	der Frostschutz
antiseptic	das Antiseptikum
any *(with singular)*	irgendein(e)
I haven't any	*ich habe keines*

apartment	das Appartement
appendicitis	die Blinddarmentzündung
apple	der Apfel
appointment	der Termin
(job)	die Stelle
approximately	ungefähr
apricot	die Aprikose
are	see **(to be)** GRAMMAR
arm	der Arm
arrange	vereinbaren
arrival	die Ankunft
arrive	ankommen
art gallery	die Kunsthalle
arthritis	die Arthritis
artichoke	die Artischocke
ashtray	der Aschenbecher
asparagus	der Spargel
aspirin	das Aspirin
asthma	das Asthma
at	bei
at home	*zu Hause*
aubergine	die Aubergine
auction	die Auktion
aunt	die Tante
Austria	Österreich
Austrian	österreichisch
(person) m/f	der/die Österreicher(in)
author *m/f*	der/die Autor(in)
automatic	automatisch
autumn	der Herbst
avalanche	die Lawine
avocado	die Avocado
avoid *(obstacle)*	vermeiden
awake	wach

baby	das Baby
baby food	die Babynahrung
babysitter *m/f*	der/die Babysitter(in)
back *(of body, hand)*	der Rücken
back up *vb (computer)*	sichern
bacon	der Speck
bad	schlecht
bag	die Tasche
(suitcase)	der Koffer
baggage	das Gepäck
baggage reclaim	die Gepäckausgabe
baker's	die Bäckerei
balcony	der Balkon
bald *(person)*	kahl
(tyre)	abgefahren
ball *(dance, sphere)*	der Ball
ballet	das Ballett
banana	die Banane
band *(musical)*	die Band
bandage	der Verband
bank	die Bank
bankrupt *adj*	bankrott
bar *(place)*	die Bar
barber	der (Herren)friseur
bargain	das Sonderangebot
bark *vb (dog)*	bellen
basket	der Korb
Basle	Basel
bath	das Bad
bathing cap	die Badekappe
bathroom	das Badezimmer
battery	die Batterie
be	sein *see* **(to be)** GRAMMAR
beach	der Strand

bean	die Bohne
beard	der Bart
beautiful	schön
bed	das Bett
bedding	das Bettzeug
bedroom	das Schlafzimmer
beef	das Rindfleisch
beer	das Bier
beetroot	die Rote Bete
before	vor
beggar *m/f*	der/die Bettler(in)
begin	beginnen
behind	hinter
believe	glauben
bell *(in church)*	die Glocke
(on door)	die Klingel
belong to	gehören
below	unterhalb
belt	der Gürtel
beside *(next to)*	neben
best: best wishes!	*alles Gute!*
the best	*der/die/das beste*
better	besser
between	zwischen
bicycle	das Fahrrad
big	groß
bigger	größer
bikini	der Bikini
bill *(account)*	die Rechnung
bill *vb*	fakturieren
bin	der Mülleimer
binoculars	das Fernglas
bird	der Vogel
birth	die Geburt

107

birthday	der Geburtstag
happy birthday!	*alles Gute zum Geburtstag!*
birthday card	die Geburtstagskarte
bit (piece)	das Stück
a bit (a little)	ein bißchen
bite	beißen
(insect)	stechen
bitten (by insect)	gestochen
bitter	bitter
black	schwarz
black ice	das Glatteis
blackcurrants	die schwarzen Johannisbeeren (pl)
blanket	die Decke
bleach	das Bleichmittel
blind adj	blind
blister	die Blase
blocked	verstopft
blood	das Blut
blood group	die Blutgruppe
blouse	die Bluse
blow-dry	fönen
blue	blau
boarding card	die Bordkarte
boarding house	die Pension
boat	das Boot
(ship)	das Schiff
boat trip	die Bootsfahrt
boil n	kochen
book n	das Buch
book of tickets	das Fahrscheinheft
book vb	buchen
booking (in hotel)	die Reservierung
booking office	die Vorverkaufsstelle
bookshop	die Buchhandlung

boot	der Stiefel
(of car)	der Kofferraum
border (frontier)	die Grenze
boring	langweilig
born	geboren
I was born in 1960	ich bin 1960 geboren
both	beide
bottle	die Flasche
bottle opener	der Flaschenöffner
box (container)	die Kiste
box office	die Kasse
boy	der Junge
boyfriend	der Freund
bra	der Büstenhalter
bracelet	das Armband
brake fluid	die Bremsflüssigkeit
brakes	die Bremsen (pl)
brand	die Marke
brandy	der Kognak
bread	das Brot
break (object)	kaputtmachen
breakable	zerbrechlich
breakdown	die Panne
breakdown van	der Abschleppwagen
breakfast	das Frühstück
breast	die Brust
breathe	atmen
bridge	die Brücke
briefcase	die Aktentasche
bring	bringen
Britain	Großbritannien
British	britisch
brochure	die Broschüre
broken down	kaputt

brooch	die Brosche
brother	der Bruder
brown	braun
brush	die Bürste
(for sweeping floor)	der Besen
bucket	der Eimer
buffet	das Büfett
buffet car (on train)	der Speisewagen
building (house, offices)	das Gebäude
bulb (electric)	die Glühbirne
bumper (on car)	die Stoßstange
bun (cake)	das süße Brötchen
bunch of flowers	der Blumenstrauß
bureau de change	die Wechselstube
burn n (on skin)	die Brandwunde
burn vb	verbrennen
burnt (food)	angebrannt
burst	platzen
bus	der Bus
business	das Geschäft
business address	die Geschäftsadresse
bus station	der Busbahnhof
bus stop	die Bushaltestelle
bus tour	die Busfahrt
busy	beschäftigt
but	aber
butcher m/f	der/die Metzger(in)
butter	die Butter
butterfly	der Schmetterling
button	der Knopf
buy	kaufen
by (close to)	bei
(via)	über
bypass	die Umgehungsstraße

cabaret	das Kabarett
cabbage	der Kohl
cable car	die Seilbahn
cable television	das Kabelfernsehen
café	das Café
cake	der Kuchen
calculator	der Taschenrechner
call vb (shout)	rufen
(on telephone)	anrufen
call n (on telephone)	der Anruf
long-distance call	das Ferngespräch
calm (person)	ruhig
(weather)	windstill
camera	die Kamera
camp	campen
campsite	der Campingplatz
can n	die Dose
can vb (to be able)	können
I can/we can	ich kann/wir können
Canada	Kanada
Canadian	kanadisch
(person) m/f	der/die Kanadier(in)
cancel (ticket, etc.)	stornieren
cancer	der Krebs
canoe	das Kanu
canoeing	der Kanusport
can opener	der Dosenöffner
car	das Auto
carafe	die Karaffe
caravan	der Wohnwagen
carburettor	der Vergaser
card (greetings)	die (Glückwunsch-)karte
(playing)	die Spielkarte
cardphone	das Kartentelefon

cardigan	die Strickjacke
careful	vorsichtig
car ferry	die Autofähre
car park	der Parkplatz
carpet	der Teppich
carriage *(railway)*	der Wagen
carrot	die Karotte
carry *(bring)*	tragen
car wash	die Autowäsche
case *(suitcase)*	der Koffer
cash *vb (cheque)*	einlösen
cash *n*	das Bargeld
cash desk	die Kasse
cash dispenser	der Geldautomat
cashier *m/f*	der/die Kassierer(in)
casino	das Kasino
cassette	die Kassette
castle	das Schloß
(medieval fortress)	die Burg
catalogue	der Katalog
catch *(ball)*	fangen
(bus, train)	nehmen
cathedral	der Dom
Catholic	katholisch
cauliflower	der Blumenkohl
cause *vb*	verursachen
cave	die Höhle
celery	der Stangensellerie
cemetery	der Friedhof
centimetre	der Zentimeter
central	zentral
centre	das Zentrum
century	das Jahrhundert

certain (sure)	sicher
certificate	die Bescheinigung
chain	die Kette
chair	der Stuhl
chairlift	der Sessellift
chalet	das Chalet
champagne	der Champagner
change n (money)	das Wechselgeld
change vb (exchange)	wechseln
(alter)	ändern
changing room (in shop)	der Umkleideraum
(at swimming pool)	die Umkleidekabine
chapel	die Kapelle
charge (fee)	die Gebühr
charter flight	der Charterflug
cheap	billig
cheaper	billiger
cheap rate (telephone)	der Billigtarif
check (examine)	überprüfen
(passports, tickets)	kontrollieren
check in (at airport)	zum Checkin gehen
(at hotel)	sich an der Rezeption anmelden
check-in desk	der Abfertigungsschalter
cheerio	tschüs!
cheers (toast)	Prost!
cheese	der Käse
chemist's	die Drogerie
(for medicines)	die Apotheke
cheque	der Scheck
cheque book	das Scheckheft
cheque card	die Scheckkarte
cherries	die Kirschen (pl)
chestnut (tree)	der Kastanienbaum
(nut)	die Kastanie

chewing gum	der Kaugummi
chicken	das Hähnchen
chicken pox	die Windpocken
child	das Kind
children	die Kinder (pl)
chips (French fries)	die Pommes frites (pl)
chocolate	die Schokolade
chocolates	die Pralinen (pl)
Christmas	Weihnachten
merry Christmas!	frohe Weihnachten!
church	die Kirche
cider	der Apfelwein
cigar	die Zigarre
cigarette	die Zigarette
cigarette papers	die Zigarettenpapiere (pl)
cinema	das Kino
circus	der Zirkus
city	die Stadt
clean adj	sauber
clean vb	säubern
cleansing cream	die Reinigungscreme
client m/f	der Kunde/die Kundin
cliff	der Felsen
climbing	das Bergsteigen
climbing boots	die Bergschuhe (pl)
cloakroom	die Garderobe
clock	die Uhr
close adj (near)	nahe
close vb	schließen
closed	geschlossen
cloth	der Lappen
clothes	die Kleider (pl)
clothes peg	die Wäscheklammer

cloves	die Gewürznelken *(pl)*
club	der Club
coach *(bus)*	der Bus
coach trip	die Busreise
coast	die Küste
coastguard	die Küstenwache
coat	der Mantel
coat hanger	der Kleiderbügel
cocktail	der Cocktail
cocoa	der Kakao
coconut	die Kokosnuß
coffee	der Kaffee
white coffee	*Kaffee mit Milch*
black coffee	*schwarzer Kaffee*
coin	die Münze
Coke®	das Cola
colander	das Sieb
cold *n (illness)*	die Erkältung
cold *adj*	kalt
I'm cold	*mir ist kalt*
colleague *m/f*	der Kollege/die Kollegin
Cologne	Köln
colour	die Farbe
comb	der Kamm
come	kommen
(arrive)	ankommen
come back	zurückkommen
come in	hereinkommen
come in!	*herein!*
comfortable	bequem
commercial *n*	die Werbung
compact disk	die CD
company	die Gesellschaft
compartment	das Abteil

complain	sich beschweren
complaint	die Klage
compulsory	obligatorisch
computer	der Computer
concert	das Konzert
conditioner *(for hair)*	die Haarkur
condoms	die Kondome *(pl)*
conference	die Konferenz
conference room	das Konferenzzimmer
confession	die Konfession
confirm	bestätigen
confirmation *(flight, etc.)*	die Bestätigung
congratulations!	herzliche Glückwünsche!
connect	verbinden
connection *(train, etc.)*	die Verbindung
constipated	verstopft
consulate	das Konsulat
contact *vb*	sich in Verbindung setzen mit
contact lens cleaner	die Kontaktlinsenreiniger
contact lenses	die Kontaktlinsen *(pl)*
contraceptive	das Verhütungsmittel
cook	kochen
cooker	der Herd
cool	kühl
copy *n*	die Kopie
copy *vb*	kopieren
corkscrew	der Korkenzieher
corner	die Ecke
cost	kosten
cotton	die Baumwolle
cotton wool	die Watte
couchette	der Liegewagen
cough	der Husten

country	das Land
couple (pair)	das Paar
courgettes	die Zucchini (pl)
course (of meal)	der Gang
cover charge	der Preis für ein Gedeck
crab	die Krabbe
crash (noise)	das Krachen
(collision)	der Zusammenstoß
crash helmet	der Sturzhelm
cream (lotion)	die Creme
(on milk)	die Sahne
credit card	die Kreditkarte
crisps	die Chips (pl)
croquette	die Krokette
cross (road)	überqueren
crossed line	gestörte Leitung
crossroads	die Kreuzung
crowded (full)	überfüllt
cruise	die Kreuzfahrt
cucumber	die Gurke
cup	die Tasse
cupboard	der Schrank
currant	die Korinthe
current (electric)	der Strom
curtain	der Vorhang
cushion	das Kissen
custard	die Vanillesoße
customer m/f	der Kunde/die Kundin
customs	der Zoll
cut n	die Schnittwunde
cut vb	schneiden
cutlery	das Besteck
cycle vb	radfahren
cycling	das Radfahren

daily *(each day)*	täglich
damage	der Schaden
damp	feucht
dance *n*	der Tanz
dance *vb*	tanzen
dangerous	gefährlich
dark	dunkel
date	das Datum
date of birth	das Geburtsdatum
daughter	die Tochter
day	der Tag
dear	lieb
(expensive)	teuer
decaffeinated	koffeinfrei
deck chair	der Liegestuhl
declare	erklären
deep	tief
deep freeze	die Tiefkühltruhe
defrost	entfrosten
de-ice	enteisen
delay	die Verspätung
delayed	verspätet
delicious	köstlich
dentist *m/f*	der Zahnarzt/die Zahnärztin
dentures	das Gebiß
deodorant	das Deodorant
department store	das Kaufhaus
departure	die Abfahrt
departure lounge	die Abflughalle
deposit	die Anzahlung
dessert	der Nachtisch
details	die Details *(pl)*
detergent	das Reinigungsmittel

detour	der Umweg
develop	entwickeln
diabetic *m/f*	der/die Diabetiker(in)
dialling code	die Vorwahl
dialling tone	der Wählton
diamond	der Diamant
diarrhoea	der Durchfall
diary	das Tagebuch
dictionary	das Wörterbuch
diesel	das Dieselöl
diet *(slimming)*	die Abmagerungskur
(special)	die Diät
different	verschieden
difficult	schwierig
dinghy	das Dingi
dining room	das Eßzimmer
dinner *(lunch)*	das Mittagessen
(evening meal)	das Abendessen
direct *(route, train)*	direkt
directory enquiries	die Auskunft
dirty	schmutzig
disabled	behindert
disco	die Disko
discount	der Rabatt
dish	die Schale
(food)	das Gericht
dishtowel	das Abtrockentuch
dishwasher	die Geschirrspülmaschine
disk *(computer)*	die Diskette
disk drive	das Diskettenlaufwerk
disinfectant	das Desinfektionsmittel
distilled water	das destillierte Wasser
divorced	geschieden
dizzy	schwindelig

do	machen
I do	*ich mache*
doctor *m/f*	der Arzt/die Ärztin
dollar	der Dollar
domestic *(flight, etc)*	Inland
door	die Tür
double	Doppel-
double bed	das Doppelbett
double room	das Doppelzimmer
down *(to go downstairs)*	heruntergehen
downstairs	unten
draught *(in room)*	der Durchzug
dress *n*	das Kleid
dress *vb (to get dressed)*	sich anziehen
dressing *(for food)*	die Soße
drink *n*	das Getränk
drink *vb*	trinken
drinking chocolate	die heiße Schokolade
drinking water	das Trinkwasser
drive	fahren
driver *(of car) m/f*	der Fahrer/die Fahrerin
driving licence	der Führerschein
drunk	betrunken
dry *adj*	trocken
dry *vb*	trocknen
dry cleaner's	die Reinigung
duck	die Ente
due: *when's it due?*	*wann soll es ankommen?*
dummy *(for baby)*	der Schnuller
during	während
duty-free	duty-free
duty-free shop	der Duty-free-Shop
duvet	die Bettdecke

each	jede(r/s)
ear	das Ohr
earache	die Ohrenschmerzen
I have earache	*ich habe Ohrenschmerzen*
earlier	früher
early	früh
earn *(money, praise)*	verdienen
earrings	die Ohrringe *(pl)*
earth	die Erde
earthquake	das Erdbeben
east	der Osten
Easter	Ostern
easy	leicht
eat	essen
EC	die EG
economic	ökonomisch
economy	die Wirtschaft
economy class	die Touristenklasse
eel	der Aal
eggs	die Eier *(pl)*
fried egg	*das Spiegelei*
hard-boiled egg	*das hartgekochte Ei*
scrambled egg	*das Rührei*
either	eine(r/s) (von beiden)
elastic	elastisch
elastic band	das Gummiband
electric	elektrisch
electrician *m/f*	der/die Elektriker(in)
electricity	die Elektrizität
electricity meter	der Stromzähler
electric razor	der Elektrorasierer
embassy	die Botschaft
emergency	der Notfall
empty	leer

end	das Ende
engaged *(to be married)*	verlobt
(toilet, telephone)	besetzt
engine	der Motor
England	England
English	englisch
(person) m/f	der/die Engländer(in)
enjoy: *I enjoyed it*	*es hat mir gefallen*
I enjoy swimming	*ich schwimme gern*
enough	genug
enquiry desk	die Auskunft
entrance	der Eingang
entrance fee	das Eintrittsgeld
envelope	der Umschlag
environment	die Umwelt
equipment	die Ausrüstung
escalator	die Rolltreppe
especially	besonders
essential	wesentlich
Eurocheque	der Euroscheck
Europe	Europa
evening	der Abend
in the evening	*am Abend*
every *(each)*	jede(r/s)
everyone	jeder
everything	alles
excellent	ausgezeichnet
except	außer
excess luggage	das Übergewicht
exchange n	der Austausch
exchange vb	tauschen
(money)	wechseln
exchange rate	der Wechselkurs
exciting	aufregend

excursion	der Ausflug
excuse	entschuldigen
excuse me! *(sorry)*	*Entschuldigung*
(when passing)	*entschuldigen Sie bitte*
exhaust pipe	das Auspuffrohr
exhibition	die Ausstellung
exit	der Ausgang
expect	erwarten
expenses	die Spesen
expensive	teuer
expert *m/f*	der Experte/die Expertin
expire *(ticket, passport)*	ungültig werden
explain	erklären
express *n (train)*	der Schnellzug
express *adj (parcel, etc)*	per Expreß
extension *(telephone)*	der Apparat
extension cable	das Verlängerungskabel
extra *(spare)*	übrig
(more)	noch ein(e)
eye	das Auge
eye liner	der Eyeliner
eye shadow	der Lidschatten

fabric	der Stoff
face	das Gesicht
facilities	die Einrichtungen *(pl)*
factory	die Fabrik
faint: she has fainted	sie ist in Ohnmacht gefallen
fair *(trade fair)*	die Messe
(funfair)	die Kirmes
fall	fallen
false teeth	das Gebiß
family	die Familie

famous	berühmt
fan (electric)	der Ventilator
fan belt	der Keilriemen
far	weit
fare	der Fahrpreis
farm	der Bauernhof
farmhouse	das Bauernhaus
fast	schnell
fat	dick
father	der Vater
fault (defect)	der Fehler
it wasn't my fault	das war nicht meine Schuld
favourite	Lieblings-
fax n	das Fax
fax vb	faxen
fax machine	das Fax
fax number	die Faxnummer
feed	füttern
feel	fühlen
I don't feel well	ich fühle mich nicht wohl
I feel sick	mir ist schlecht
fees	das Honorar
ferry	die Fähre
festival	das Fest
fetch (bring)	holen
fever	das Fieber
few: a few	ein paar
fiancé(e)	der/die Verlobte
field	das Feld
file (nail)	die Feile
(computer)	die Datei
fill	füllen
(fill up petrol tank)	volltanken
fillet	das Filet

filling *(in tooth)*	die Plombe
film	der Film
filter	der Filter
filter-tipped	Filter-
financial year	das Geschäftsjahr
finish	beenden
fire	das Feuer
fire brigade	die Feuerwehr
fire escape	die Feuertreppe
fire extinguisher	der Feuerlöscher
fireplace	der Kamin
first	erste(r/s)
first aid	die Erste Hilfe
first class *(travel)*	erster Klasse
first floor	die erste Etage
first name	der Vorname
fish *n*	der Fisch
fish *vb*	fischen
fishing rod	die Angelrute
fit *n (seizure)*	der Anfall
fit *vb*	passen
fix	reparieren
fizzy	sprudelnd
flash	das Blitzlicht
flask	die Thermosflasche
flat *(apartment)*	die Wohnung
flat tyre	die Reifenpanne
flavour	der Geschmack
flight	der Flug
flood	die Flut
floor *(of building)*	die Etage
(of room)	der Boden
floppy disk	die Floppy-disk

flour	das Mehl
flowers	die Blumen
flu	die Grippe
fly sheet	das Überzelt
foggy	neblig
foil *(tinfoil)*	die Alufolie
fold *(clothes)*	zusammenlegen
folder	der Aktendeckel
follow	folgen
font *(typeface)*	die Schrift
food	das Essen
food poisoning	die Lebensmittelvergiftung
foot	der Fuß
on foot	*zu Fuß*
football	der Fußball
footpath	der Fußweg
for	für
forbidden	verboten
foreign	ausländisch
foreigner *m/f*	der/die Ausländer(in)
forest	der Wald
forget	vergessen
forgive	vergeben
fork *(at table)*	die Gabel
(in road)	die Gabelung
form	die Form
fortnight	zwei Wochen
fountain	der Brunnen
fox	der Fuchs
fracture	der Bruch
fragile	zerbrechlich
France	Frankreich
free *(not occupied)*	frei
(costing nothing)	umsonst

freezer	die Tiefkühltruhe
freight	die Fracht
French	französisch
(person) m/f	der Franzose/die Französin
French beans	die grünen Bohnen
frequent	häufig
fresh	frisch
fridge	der Kühlschrank
fried	gebraten ; Brat-
friend m/f	der/die Freund(in)
friendly	freundlich
from	von
front	die Vorderseite
frozen	gefroren
fruit	das Obst
fruit juice	der Fruchtsaft
fruit salad	der Obstsalat
frying-pan	die Bratpfanne
fuel (petrol)	das Benzin
fuel pump	die Benzinpumpe
full	voll
full board	die Vollpension
fully booked	ausgebucht
funeral	die Beerdigung
funfair	die Kirmes
funny (amusing)	lustig
(odd)	komisch
fur	der Pelz
furious	wütend
furnished	möbliert
furniture	die Möbel
further on	weiter
fuse	die Sicherung
future	die Zukunft

gallery	die Galerie
gallon	= approx. 4.5 litres
game	das Spiel
garage	die Werkstatt
garden	der Garten
garlic	der Knoblauch
gas	das Gas
gas cylinder	die Gasflasche
gears	das Getriebe
gents (toilet)	Herrentoilette
genuine	echt
German	deutsch
(person) m/f	der/die Deutsche
German measles	die Röteln
Germany	Deutschland
get (receive, obtain)	bekommen
(fetch)	holen
get into (bus, etc.)	einsteigen
get out of (vehicle)	aussteigen
gift	das Geschenk
gin	der Gin
girl	das Mädchen
girlfriend	die Freundin
give	geben
glass	das Glas
glasses	die Brille
gloves	die Handschuhe
glue	der Klebstoff
go	gehen
go back	zurückgehen
go in	hineingehen
go out	hinausgehen
goggles (for swimming)	die Taucherbrille
(for skiing)	die Schneebrille

gold	golden
golf	das Golf
golf course	der Golfplatz
good	gut
(pleasant)	schön
good afternoon	guten Tag
goodbye	auf Wiedersehen
good evening	guten Abend
good morning	guten Morgen
good night	gute Nacht
gramme	das Gramm
grandfather	der Großvater
grandmother	die Großmutter
grapefruit	die Grapefruit
grapefruit juice	der Grapefruitsaft
grapes	die Trauben (pl)
greasy	fettig
green	grün
green card (insurance)	die grüne Versicherungskarte
grey	grau
grilled	gegrillt
grocer's (shop)	der Lebensmittelladen
ground	der Boden
ground floor	das Erdgeschoß
groundsheet	der Zeltboden
group	die Gruppe
guarantee	die Garantie
guard m/f	der/die Schaffner(in)
guest	der Gast
guesthouse	die Pension
guide (tour guide) m/f	der/die Fremdenführer(in)
guidebook	der Führer
guided tour	die Fremdenführung

haemorrhoids	die Hämorrhoiden (pl)
hair	die Haare (pl)
hairbrush	die Haarbürste
haircut	der Haarschnitt
hairdresser m/f	der Friseur/die Friseuse
hairdryer	der Fön
hairgrip	die Haarklemme
hair spray	das Haarspray
half	halb
a half bottle	eine kleine Flasche
half board	die Halbpension
half fare	der halbe Fahrpreis
ham	der Schinken
hand	die Hand
handbag	die Handtasche
handicapped	behindert
handkerchief	das Taschentuch
handle	der Griff
hand luggage	das Handgepäck
hand-made	handgearbeitet
hangover	der Kater
hang up (telephone)	auflegen
Hanover	Hannover
happen	geschehen ; passieren
what happened?	was ist passiert?
happy	glücklich
harbour	der Hafen
hard	hart
hat	der Hut
have	haben see GRAMMAR
hay fever	der Heuschnupfen
he	er see GRAMMAR
head	der Kopf
headache	die Kopfschmerzen (pl)

headphones	die Kopfhörer *(pl)*
health food shop	das Reformhaus
healthy	gesund
hear	hören
heart	das Herz
heart attack	der Herzanfall
heater	das Heizgerät
heating	die Heizung
heavy	schwer
hello	hallo
help *n*	die Hilfe
help!	*Hilfe!*
help *vb*	helfen
can you help me?	*können Sie mir helfen?*
herbs	die Kräuter *(pl)*
here	hier
hide	verstecken
high	hoch
(number, speed)	groß
high blood pressure	der hohe Blutdruck
high chair	der Kinderstuhl
high tide	die Flut
hill	der Hügel
hill-walking	das Bergwandern
hip	die Hüfte
hire	mieten
hit	schlagen
hitchhike	trampen
hold	halten
(contain)	enthalten
hold-up *(traffic jam)*	der Stau
hole	das Loch
holiday	der Feiertag
on holiday	*in den Ferien*

holy	heilig
home	das Zuhause
homesick (to be)	*Heimweh haben*
honey	der Honig
honeymoon	die Flitterwochen (pl)
hope	hoffen
I hope so/not	*hoffentlich/hoffentlich nicht*
horn (car)	die Hupe
hors d'oeuvre	die Vorspeise
horse	das Pferd
hose	der Schlauch
hospital	das Krankenhaus
hot	heiß
I'm hot	*mir ist heiß*
it's hot (weather)	*es ist heiß*
hotel	das Hotel
hour	die Stunde
house	das Haus
house wine	der Hauswein
housework	die Hausarbeit
hovercraft	das Luftkissenboot
how	wie
how much?	*wieviel*
how many?	*wieviele*
how are you?	*wie geht es Ihnen?*
huge	riesig
hundred	hundert
hungry: I'm hungry	*ich habe Hunger*
hunt	jagen
hurry: I'm in a hurry	*ich habe es eilig*
hurt (feel pain)	schmerzen
my back hurts	*mir tut der Rücken weh*
husband	der Mann
hydrofoil	das Tragflügelboot

I	ich *see* **GRAMMAR**
ice	das Eis
ice cream	das Eis
iced	eisgekühlt
ice rink	die Schlittschuhbahn
if	wenn
ignition	die Zündung
ill	krank
immediately	sofort
important	wichtig
impossible	unmöglich
in *(place, position)*	in
inch	= *approx. 2.5 cm*
included	inbegriffen
indigestion	die Magenverstimmung
indoors	drinnen
(at home)	zu Hause
infection	die Infektion
infectious	ansteckend
information	die Auskunft
information office	das Informationsbüro
injection	die Spritze
injured *(person)*	verletzt
injury	die Verletzung
ink	die Tinte
insect	das Insekt
insect bite	der (Insekten)stich
insect repellent	das Insektenschutzmittel
inside	in
insist on	bestehen auf
install	installieren
instalment	die Rate
instant coffee	der Pulverkaffee

instead	stattdessen
instructor *(ski) m/f*	der/die Skilehrer(in)
insulin	das Insulin
insurance	die Versicherung
insurance certificate	die Versicherungsbescheinigung
interesting	interessant
interest rate	der Zinssatz
international	international
(arrivals, departures)	Ausland
interpreter *m/f*	der/die Dolmetscher(in)
interrupt	unterbrechen
interval *(play)*	die Pause
interview	das Interview
into	in
introduce	vorstellen
invent	erfinden
invitation	die Einladung
invite	einladen
invoice	die Rechnung
Ireland	Irland
Irish	irisch
(person) m/f	der Ire/die Irin
iron *(for clothes)*	das Bügeleisen
iron *vb*	bügeln
ironmonger's	die Eisenwarenhandlung
is	see **(to be)** GRAMMAR
island	die Insel
it	er/sie/es see GRAMMAR
Italian	italienisch
(person) m/f	der/die Italiener(in)
Italy	Italien
itch	das Jucken
itinerary	die Reiseroute

English	German
jack *(for car)*	der Wagenheber
jacket	die Jacke
jam *(food)*	die Marmelade
jammed *(camera, lock)*	blockiert
jar	das Gefäß
jaundice	die Gelbsucht
jaw	der Kiefer
jazz	der Jazz
jeans	die Jeans
jelly *(dessert)*	die (rote) Grütze
jellyfish	die Qualle
jersey	der Pullover
jeweller's	der Juwelier
jewellery	der Schmuck
Jewish	jüdisch
job *(employment)*	die Stelle
jog *vb*	joggen
join *(things together)*	verbinden
(club)	beitreten
joke	der Witz
journalist *m/f*	der/die Journalist(in)
journey	die Reise
joy	die Freude
judge *m/f*	der/die Richter(in)
jug	der Krug
juice	der Saft
jump	springen
jump leads	die Starthilfekabel
junction *(roads)*	die Kreuzung
jungle	der Dschungel
just: *just two*	*nur zwei*
I've just arrived	*ich bin gerade angekommen*

keep	behalten
keep the change!	*stimmt so!*
kennel	die Hundehütte
kettle	der Wasserkocher
key	der Schlüssel
(typewriter, computer)	die Taste
keyboard	die Tastatur
key in	eingeben
keyring	der Schlüsselring
keystroke	der Anschlag
kick *n*	der Stoss
kick *vb (ball)*	schießen
(person)	treten
kidneys	die Nieren *(pl)*
kill	töten
kilo	das Kilo
kilometre	der Kilometer
kind *n (sort, type)*	die Art
kind *adj (person)*	nett
king	der König
kiss *n*	der Kuß
kiss *vb*	küssen
kitchen	die Küche
kitten	das Kätzchen
knee	das Knie
knickers	der Slip
knife	das Messer
knit	stricken
knitting needle	die Stricknadel
knock *(strike, bump into)*	stoßen
(on door)	klopfen
knot	der Knoten
know *(facts)*	wissen
(be acquainted with)	kennen

label	das Schild
lace (of shoe)	der Schnürsenkel
(fabric)	die Spitze
ladder	die Leiter
ladies (toilet)	die Damentoilette
lady	die Dame
lager	das helle Bier
lake	der See
lamb	das Lammfleisch
lamp (for table)	die Lampe
(in street)	die Straßenlampe
land n	das Land
land vb	landen
lane (small country road)	das Sträßchen
(of motorway/main road)	die Spur
large	groß
last (final)	letzte(r/s)
last week	letzte Woche
late	spät
the train is late	der Zug hat Verspätung
sorry we're late	es tut uns leid, daß wir zu spät sind
later	später
launderette	der Waschsalon
laundry service	der Wäschereiservice
lavatory	die Toilette
lawyer m/f	der Rechtsanwalt/die Rechtsanwältin
laxative	das Abführmittel
layby	die Haltebucht
lazy	faul
lead n (electric)	das Kabel
lead vb	führen
leader m/f	der/die Führer(in)
leaf	das Blatt

leak (of gas, liquid)	das Leck
learn	lernen
least: at least	*mindestens*
leather	das Leder
leave (leave behind)	zurücklassen
when does the train leave?	*wann fährt der Zug ab?*
left: on/to the left	*links/nach links*
left-luggage locker	das Schließfach
left-luggage office	die Gepäckaufbewahrung
leg	das Bein
lemon	die Zitrone
lemonade	die Limonade
lemon tea	der Zitronentee
lend	leihen
length (size)	die Länge
(duration)	die Dauer
lens	die Linse
lentils	die Linsen (pl)
less	weniger
less milk	*weniger Milch*
lesson	die Unterrichtsstunde
let (allow)	erlauben
(room, house)	vermieten
letter (written)	der Brief
letter box	der Briefkasten
lettuce	der Kopfsalat
level (flat)	eben
library	die Bibliothek
licence (driving licence)	der Führerschein
(for gun)	der Waffenschein
lick	lecken
lid	der Deckel
lie down	sich hinlegen

life	das Leben
lifeboat	das Rettungsschiff
lifeguard *m/f*	der/die Rettungsschwimmer(in)
life jacket	die Schwimmweste
lift	der Aufzug
lift pass *(on ski slopes)*	der Liftpaß
light	das Licht
have you a light?	*können Sie mir Feuer geben?*
light bulb	die Glühbirne
lighter	das Feuerzeug
lightning	der Blitz
like *prep*	*wie*
like you	*wie Sie*
like this	*so*
like *vb*	*mögen*
I like coffee	*ich trinke gern Kaffee*
I'd like a newspaper	*ich möchte eine Zeitung*
likely	wahrscheinlich
lime *(fruit)*	die Limone
line *(row, of railway)*	die Linie
(queue)	die Schlange
(telephone)	die Leitung
(of typed text)	die Zeile
lip salve	die Lippenpomade
lipstick	der Lippenstift
liqueur	der Likör
list	die Liste
listen to	horchen
litre	der Liter
little: *a little milk*	*ein bißchen Milch*
live *(exist)*	leben
(reside)	wohnen
I live in London	*ich wohne in London*
liver	die Leber
living room	das Wohnzimmer

139

loaf	das Brot
lobster	der Hummer
local *(wine, speciality)*	hiesig
lock *vb*	zuschließen
lock *n (on door, box)*	das Schloß
London	London
long	lang
for a long time	*lange Zeit*
look	schauen
look after	sich kümmern um
look for	suchen
lorry	der Lastwagen
lose	verlieren
lost *(object)*	verloren
I've lost my wallet	*ich habe meine Brieftasche verloren*
I'm lost *(on foot)*	*ich habe mich verlaufen*
I'm lost *(in car)*	*ich habe mich verfahren*
lost property office	das Fundbüro
lot: a lot	viel
lotion	die Lotion
loud	laut
lounge *(in hotel)*	der Aufenthaltsraum
love	lieben
I love swimming	*ich schwimme sehr gern*
lovely	hübsch
low	niedrig
(standard, quality)	minderwertig
lucky	glücklich
luggage	das Gepäck
luggage allowance	das Höchstgewicht
luggage rack	die Gepäckablage
luggage tag	der Kofferanhänger
luggage trolley	der Gepäckwagen
lunch	das Mittagessen

macaroni	die Makkaroni *(pl)*
machine	die Maschine
mad	verrückt
madam	gnädige Frau
magazine	die Zeitschrift
maid *(in hotel)*	das Zimmermädchen
maiden name	der Mädchenname
main	Haupt-
main course	das Hauptgericht
main road	die Hauptstraße
mains *(switch)*	der Hauptschalter
make	machen
(meal)	zubereiten
make-up *(cosmetics)*	das Make-up
male	männlich
mallet	der Holzhammer
man	der Mann
manage *(direct)*	leiten
(cope)	schaffen
manager *m/f*	der/die Geschäftsführer(in)
managing director *m/f*	der/die Direktor(in)
many	viele
map	die Karte
marble	der Marmor
margarine	die Margarine
mark *(stain)*	der Fleck
market	der Markt
marmalade	die Orangenmarmelade
married	verheiratet
marry *(get married)*	heiraten
mascara	die Wimperntusche
mashed potato	das Kartoffelpüree
Mass *(in church)*	die Messe

match *(sport)*	der Wettkampf
matches	die Streichhölzer *(pl)*
material	der Stoff
matter: *no matter!*	*macht nichts!*
what's the matter?	*was ist los?*
mayonnaise	die Mayonnaise
me *(direct object)*	mich
(indirect object)	mir
meal	das Essen
mean	bedeuten
what does this mean?	*was bedeutet das?*
measles	die Masern *(pl)*
measure	messen
meat	das Fleisch
mechanic *m/f*	der/die Mechaniker(in)
media	die Medien *pl*
medical insurance	die Krankenversicherung
medicine	die Medizin
medium	mittlere(r/s)
medium rare	halb durch
meet *(by accident)*	treffen
(by arrangement)	sich treffen
meeting	das Treffen
melon	die Melone
member	das Mitglied
men	die Männer *(pl)*
menu	die Speisekarte
message	die Nachricht
metal	das Metall
meter	der Zähler
metre	der Meter
midday	der Mittag
middle	die Mitte
middle-aged	in den mittleren Jahren

midnight	die Mitternacht
migraine	die Migräne
milk	die Milch
milkshake	das Milchmixgetränk
millimetre	der Millimeter
million	die Million
mince	das Hackfleisch
mind: do you mind if...?	haben Sie etwas dagegen, wenn...?
I don't mind	es ist mir egal
mineral water	das Mineralwasser
minimum	das Minimum
minister (in church)	der/die Pfarrer(in)
minor road	die Nebenstraße
mint (herb)	die Minze
(sweet)	das Pfefferminz
minute	die Minute
mirror	der Spiegel
miss (train, etc)	verpassen
Miss	Fräulein
missing (object)	verschwunden
my son's missing	mein Sohn ist weg
mistake	der Fehler
misty	dunstig
misunderstanding	das Mißverständnis
there's been a misunderstanding	wir haben uns mißverstanden
mixed	gemischt
modern	modern
moisturizer	die Feuchtigkeitscreme
monastery	das Kloster
money	das Geld
money order	die Postanweisung
monkey m/f	der Affe/die Äffin
month	der Monat

monthly	monatlich
monument	das Monument
mop *(for floor)*	der Mop
more	mehr
more wine, please	noch etwas Wein, bitte
morning	der Morgen
mosque	die Moschee
mosquito	die Stechmücke
most: most of	*das meiste*
mother	die Mutter
motor	der Motor
motor boat	das Motorboot
motor cycle	das Motorrad
motorway	die Autobahn
mountain	der Berg
mouse	die Maus
mousse	die Creme(speise)
moustache	der Schnurrbart
mouth	der Mund
move	bewegen
I can't move my leg	*ich kann mein Bein nicht bewegen*
Mr	Herr
Mrs	Frau
much	viel
it costs too much	*es kostet zuviel*
Munich	München
museum	das Museum
mushrooms	die Pilze *(pl)*
music	die Musik
mussel	die Muschel
must	müssen
mustard	der Senf
mutton	das Hammelfleisch
my	mein

nail	der Nagel
nail polish	der Nagellack
nail polish remover	der Nagellackentferner
naked	nackt
name	der Name
napkin	die Serviette
nappy	die Windel
narrow	eng
nationality	die Nationalität
navy blue	marineblau
near (place, time)	nahe
necessary	notwendig
neck	der Hals
necklace	die Halskette
need	brauchen
I need an aspirin	*ich brauche ein Aspirin*
I need to go	*ich muß gehen*
needle	die Nadel
needle and thread	*Nadel und Faden*
negative (photography)	das Negativ
neighbour (male)	der/die Nachbar(in)
nephew	der Neffe
nest	das Nest
nettle	die Nessel
network	das Netz
never	nie
I never drink wine	*Wein trinke ich nie*
new	neu
news	die Nachrichten
newsagent's m/f	der/die Zeitungshändler(in)
newspaper	die Zeitung
New Year	das neue Jahr
happy New Year!	*ein gutes Neues Jahr*
New Zealand	Neuseeland

next	nächste(r/s)
the next stop	*die nächste Haltestelle*
next week	*nächste Woche*
nice *(person)*	nett
(pleasant)	angenehm
niece	die Nichte
night	die Nacht
at night	*nachts*
night club	der Nachtklub
nightdress	das Nachthemd
no	nein
no thank you	*nein danke*
nobody	niemand
noisy	laut
non-alcoholic	nichtalkoholisch
none	keine(r/s)
there's none left	*es ist nichts übrig*
non-smoking	Nichtraucher-
north	der Norden
Northern Ireland	Nordirland
not	nicht
I don't know	*ich weiß nicht*
note *(banknote)*	der Geldschein
(letter)	der kurze Brief
note pad	der Notizblock
nothing	nichts
now	jetzt
nudist beach	der FKK-Strand
number	die Zahl
Nuremberg	Nürnberg
nurse *(female)*	die Krankenschwester
(male)	der Krankenpfleger
nursery slope	der Anfängerhügel
nut *(to eat)*	die Nuß
(for bolt)	die Schraubenmutter

oak	die Eiche
oar	das Ruder
oats	der Hafer
object n	das Objekt
obtain	erhalten
occasionally	gelegentlich
odd (strange)	seltsam
of	von
off (not on)	aus
(rotten)	schlecht
offer	anbieten
office	das Büro
office block	das Bürogebäude
office hours	die Dienstzeit
official	offiziell
often	oft
how often?	wie oft?
oil	das Öl
oil filter	der Ölfilter
ointment	die Salbe
OK	okay
old	alt
how old are you?	wie alt bist du?
olive oil	das Olivenöl
olives	die Oliven
omelette	das Omelett(e)
on adj (light, engine)	an
on prep	auf
on the table	auf dem Tisch
once	einmal
one	ein
one-way street	die Einbahnstraße
onions	die Zwiebeln (pl)
only	nur

open *adj*	geöffnet
open *vb*	öffnen
opera	die Oper
operator	die Vermittlung
opposite	gegenüber
opposite the hotel	dem Hotel gegenüber
or	oder
orange *adj*	orange
orange *n*	die Orange
orange juice	der Orangensaft
order *n*	die Bestellung
order *vb*	bestellen
oregano	der Oregano
original	das Original
other: the other one	der/die/das andere
have you any others?	haben Sie noch andere da?
ounce	= approx. 30 g
out (light etc)	aus
she's out	sie ist nicht da
outdoor (pool etc)	im Freien
out of print	vergriffen
outside	draußen
oven	der Herd
over (on top of, above)	über
overbooked	übergebucht
overcharge	zuviel berechnen
overdraft	der Überziehungskredit
overnight	über Nacht
overtake (in car)	überholen
owe	schulden
I owe you ...	ich schulde Ihnen ...
owl	die Eule
owner *m/f*	der/die Besitzer(in)
oyster	die Auster

pack *(luggage)*	packen
package	das Paket
package tour	die Pauschalreise
packed lunch	das Lunchpaket
packet	das Paket
paddling pool	das Planschbecken
paid	bezahlt
painful	schmerzhaft
painkiller	das Schmerzmittel
painting	das Bild
pair	das Paar
palace	der Palast
pan *(pot)*	der Topf
pancake	der Pfannkuchen
pants *(underwear)*	der Slip
paper	das Papier
paraffin	das Paraffin
parcel	das Paket
pardon?	wie bitte?
I beg your pardon!	*Entschuldigung*
parents	die Eltern *(pl)*
park *n*	der Park
park *vb*	parken
parking disk	die Parkscheibe
parsley	die Petersilie
part	der Teil
party *(of tourists)*	die Reisegruppe
(celebration)	die Party
passenger	der Fahrgast
passport	der Reisepaß
passport control	die Paßkontrolle
pasta	die Teigwaren *(pl)*
pastry	der Teig
(cake)	das Gebäck

pâté	die Pastete
path	der Weg
pay	zahlen
payment	die Bezahlung
payphone	der Münzfernsprecher
peach	der Pfirsich
peak rate (for phoning)	Höchsttarif
peanuts	die Erdnüsse (pl)
pear	die Birne
peas	die Erbsen (pl)
peg (for clothes)	die Wäscheklammer
pen	der Füller
pencil	der Bleistift
penicillin	das Penizillin
penknife	das Taschenmesser
pensioner m/f	der/die Rentner(in)
pepper (spice)	der Pfeffer
(red/green pepper)	die Paprikaschote
people	die Leute
per: per hour	pro Stunde
per week	pro Woche
perfect	perfekt
performance	die Vorstellung
perfume	das Parfüm
perhaps	vielleicht
period (menstruation)	die Periode
perm	die Dauerwelle
permit	die Genehmigung
person	die Person
personal call (phone)	das Privatgespräch
petrol	das Benzin
petrol station	die Tankstelle
phone	see telephone
phonecard	die Telefonkarte

photocopy n	die Fotokopie
photocopy vb	fotokopieren
photograph	das Foto
picnic	das Picknick
picture (painting)	das Bild
(photo)	das Foto
pie	die Pastete
piece	das Stück
pill	die Pille
pillow	das (Kopf)kissen
pillowcase	der (Kopf)kissenbezug
pin	die Stecknadel
pineapple	die Ananas
pink	rosa
pint	= approx. 0.5 litre
a pint of beer	eine Halbe
pipe	die Pfeife
plane	das Flugzeug
plaster (sticking plaster)	das Pflaster
plastic	das Plastik
plate	der Teller
platform (at station)	der Bahnsteig
play	spielen
playroom	das Spielzimmer
please (in polite request)	bitte
pleased	erfreut
pliers	die Zange
plug (electrical)	der Stecker
(in bath)	der Stöpsel
plum	die Pflaume
plumber m/f	der/die Installateur(in)
points (in car)	die Unterbrecherkontakte (pl)
poison	das Gift
poisonous	giftig

police	die Polizei
police!	Polizei!
policeman(-woman)	der/die Polizist(in)
police station	das Polizeirevier
polish (for shoes)	die Schuhcreme
polite	höflich
polluted	verschmutzt
pony trekking	das Ponyreiten
poor	arm
popular	beliebt
pork	das Schweinefleisch
port (seaport)	der Hafen
(wine)	der Portwein
porter	der Portier
(in station)	der Gepäckträger
portion	die Portion
possible	möglich
post	aufgeben
postbox	der Briefkasten
postcard	die Ansichtskarte
postcode	die Postleitzahl
postman m/f	der/die Briefträger(in)
post office	das Postamt
postpone	verschieben
pot (for cooking)	der Topf
potatoes	die Kartoffeln
pottery	die Tonwaren
pound	das Pfund
powdered milk	die Trockenmilch
pram	der Kinderwagen
prawn	die Garnele
prefer	vorziehen
pregnant	schwanger
prepare	vorbereiten

prescription	das Rezept
present	das Geschenk
pretty	hübsch
preview	die Vorschau
price	der Preis
price list	die Preisliste
priest	der Priester
prince	der Prinz
princess	die Prinzessin
printer *(computer)*	der Drucker
print-out *(computer)*	der Ausdruck
prison	das Gefängnis
private	privat
prize	der Preis
probably	wahrscheinlich
problem	das Problem
programme	das Programm
pronounce	aussprechen
how's it pronounced?	wie spricht man das aus?
Protestant	protestantisch
public	öffentlich
public holiday	der gesetzliche Feiertag
pudding	der Pudding
pull *(drag, draw)*	ziehen
pullover	der Pullover
puncture	die Reifenpanne
purchase order	die Bestellung
purple	violett
purse	der Geldbeutel
push	stoßen
put *(insert)*	einsetzen
put down	stellen
pyjamas	der Pyjama

quality	die Qualität
quantity	die Quantität
quarrel *n*	der Streit
quarter	das Viertel
quay	der Kai
queen	die Königin
question	die Frage
queue	die Schlange
quick	schnell
quickly	schnell
quiet	ruhig
quilt	die Bettdecke
quite *(rather)*	ziemlich
(completely)	ganz
rabbit	das Kaninchen
rabies	die Tollwut
race *(competition)*	das Rennen
(of people)	die Rasse
racket *(tennis)*	der Schläger
radio	das Radio
railway	die Eisenbahn
railway station	der Bahnhof
rain	der Regen
rainbow	der Regenbogen
raincoat	der Regenmantel
rain	der Regen
it's raining	es regnet
raisins	die Rosinen *(pl)*
ramp	die Rampe
rare *(unique)*	selten
(steak)	blutig
raspberries	die Himbeeren *(pl)*

rate (ratio)	die Rate
(price)	der Preis
rate of exchange	der Wechselkurs
raw	roh
razor	der Rasierapparat
reach	erreichen
read	lesen
ready	fertig
real	echt
realize	erkennen
reason	der Grund
receipt	die Quittung
receiver (of telephone)	der Hörer
recently	kürzlich
reception	der Empfang
recipe	das Rezept
recognize	erkennen
recommend	empfehlen
record (music)	die Schallplatte
(document)	die Unterlage
recyclable	wiederverwertbar
red	rot
reduction	die Ermäßigung
refill (for pen)	die Ersatzmine
(for lighter)	die Nachfüllpatrone
refund n	die Rückerstattung
refund vb	zurückerstatten
refurbished	renoviert
region	das Gebiet
registered (mail)	Einschreib-
registration number	das Kraftfahrzeugkennzeichen
regulation	die Regelung
reimburse	entschädigen
relation (family) m/f	der/die Verwandte

reliable (person)	zuverlässig
(secure, sound)	verläßlich
remain	bleiben
remember	sich erinnern
rent	mieten
rental (house)	die Miete
repair	reparieren
repeat	wiederholen
reply	antworten
report	der Bericht
rescue vb	retten
reservation	die Reservierung ; die Buchung
reserve	reservieren ; buchen
reserved	reserviert
rest n	die Ruhe
the rest of the wine	der Rest des Weins
rest vb	ruhen
restaurant	das Restaurant
restaurant car	der Speisewagen
return (go back)	zurückgehen
(give back)	zurückgeben
return ticket (train)	die Rückfahrkarte
(plane)	das Rückflugticket
reverse (car)	rückwärts fahren
reverse charge call	das R-Gespräch
reversing lights	die Rückfahrscheinwerfer (pl)
review (play, film, etc.)	die Kritik
rheumatism	der Rheumatismus
rice	der Reis
rich (person)	reich
(food)	mächtig
ride (horse)	reiten
(in car)	fahren
right adj	richtig

right n : on the right	rechts
to the right	nach rechts
ring	der Ring
ripe	reif
river	der Fluß
road (route)	der Weg
(street)	die Straße
road map	die Straßenkarte
roast	Rost-
roll (bread)	das Brötchen
roof	das Dach
roof-rack	der Dachträger
room (in house, hotel)	das Zimmer
(space)	der Platz
room service	der Zimmerservice
rope	das Seil
rosé	rosé
rough	rauh
round	rund
round the corner	um die Ecke
route	die Route
rowing boat	das Ruderboot
rubber (eraser)	der Radiergummi
(material)	das Gummi
rubber band	das Gummiband
rubbish	der Abfall
rucksack	der Rucksack
ruin	der Ruin
rum	der Rum
run	rennen
rush	die Hetze
rush hour	die Stoßzeit
rusty	rostig
rye bread	das Roggenbrot

saccharin	der Süßstoff
sad	traurig
safe n	der Safe
safe adj (not dangerous)	ungefährlich
safety pin	die Sicherheitsnadel
sage (herb)	der Salbei
sailboard	das Segelbrett
sailing (sport)	das Segeln
saint m/f	der/die Heilige
salad	der Salat
salad dressing	die Salatsoße
sale (in general)	der Verkauf
(bargains)	der Ausverkauf
salmon	der Lachs
salt	das Salz
salty	salzig
same	gleich
sandy (beach)	sandig
sandals	die Sandalen (pl)
sandwich	das Sandwich
sanitary towels	die Damenbinden (pl)
sardine	die Sardine
sauce	die Soße
saucepan	der Kochtopf
saucer	die Untertasse
sauna	die Sauna
sausage	die Wurst
save (person)	retten
(money)	sparen
savoury	schmackhaft
say	sagen
scales (weighing)	die Waage
scallop	die Jakobsmuschel
scampi	die Scampi (pl)

scarf *(headscarf)*	das Kopftuch
(round neck)	das Halstuch
scenery	die Landschaft
school	die Schule
scissors	die Schere
Scotland	Schottland
Scottish	schottisch
(person) m/f	der Schotte/die Schottin
scrape *(paint)*	kratzen
screen *(TV, computer)*	der Bildschirm
screw	die Schraube
screwdriver	der Schraubenzieher
sculpture	die Skulptur
sea	die See
seafood	die Meeresfrüchte *(pl)*
seasickness	die Seekrankheit
season *(of year)*	die Jahreszeit
season ticket	die Zeitkarte
seat *(chair)*	der Sitz
(in bus, train, theatre)	der Platz
seatbelt	der Sicherheitsgurt
seaweed	die Alge
second	zweite(r/s)
second class *(seat)*	zweiter Klasse
secondhand	gebraucht
see	sehen
seem	scheinen
self-catering *(flats, etc.)*	für Selbstversorger
self-service	die Selbstbedienung
sell	verkaufen
Sellotape®	der Tesafilm®
send	schicken
senior citizen *m/f*	der/die Rentner(in)
sentence	der Satz

separate (apart)	getrennt
(different)	verschieden
serious	schlimm
serve (in shop etc)	bedienen
service	die Bedienung
service charge	die Bedienung
settle (bill)	begleichen
set menu	die Tageskarte
sew	nähen
sex (male, female)	das Geschlecht
(intercourse)	der Sex
shade (of colour)	der Ton
in the shade	im Schatten
shadow	der Schatten
shallow	seicht
shampoo	das Shampoo
shandy	das Bier mit Limonade
share	teilen
sharp	scharf
shave	rasieren
shaving cream	die Rasiercreme
shaving point	die Steckdose für Rasierapparate
she	sie see GRAMMAR
sheet (on bed)	das Bettuch
shelf	das Regal
shell (sea)	die Muschel
(egg, nut)	die Schale
shellfish	die Schalentiere (pl)
shelter	der Schutz
sherry	der Sherry
ship	das Schiff
shirt	das Hemd
shock (electrical)	der Schlag
(emotional)	der Schock

shock absorber	der Stoßdämpfer
shoe	der Schuh
shoot	schießen
shop	der Laden
shopping	das Einkaufen
to go shopping	einkaufen gehen
shopping centre	das Einkaufszentrum
short	kurz
short cut	die Abkürzung
shorts	die Shorts (pl)
shout n	der Ruf
shout vb	rufen
show n	die Aufführung
show vb	zeigen
shower (bath)	die Dusche
(of rain)	der Schauer
shrimp	die Garnele
shrink	einlaufen
shut adj	geschlossen
shut vb	schließen
shutter	der Fensterladen
sick (ill)	krank
I feel sick	mir ist schlecht
sightseeing	die Besichtigung (pl)
sign	das Schild
signature	die Unterschrift
silk	die Seide
silver	silber
similar	ähnlich
simple	einfach
sing	singen
single (unmarried)	ledig
(not double)	Einzel-
(ticket)	einfach

single bed	das Einzelbett
single room	das Einzelzimmer
sink	das Spülbecken
sir	mein Herr
sister	die Schwester
sit	sitzen
size	die Größe
skates	die Schlittschuhe
skating	das Eislaufen
skating rink	die Eisbahn
ski *n*	der Ski
ski *vb*	skifahren
ski boot	der Skistiefel
skiing	das Skilaufen
ski jacket	die Skijacke
skimmed milk	die Magermilch
skin	die Haut
skin diving	das Tauchen
ski pants	die Skihose
ski pole	der Skistock
skirt	der Rock
ski run	die Abfahrt
ski suit	der Skianzug
sky	der Himmel
sledge	der Schlitten
sleep	schlafen
sleeper *(berth)*	der Schlafwagenplatz
sleeping bag	der Schlafsack
sleeping car	der Schlafwagen
sleeping pills	die Schlaftabletten
sleeve	der Ärmel
slice	die Scheibe
slide *(photograph)*	das Dia

slip	rutschen
slow	langsam
small	klein
smaller	kleiner
smell	der Geruch
(unpleasant)	der Gestank
smoke n	der Rauch
smoke vb	rauchen
smoked	geräuchert
snack bar	die Snack Bar
snail	die Schnecke
snake	die Schlange
sneeze	niesen
snore	schnarchen
snorkel	der Schnorchel
snow	der Schnee
snowed up	eingeschneit
snowing: it's snowing	es schneit
snowplough	der Schneepflug
so: so much	soviel
soap	die Seife
soap powder	das Seifenpulver
sober	nüchtern
socket (electrical)	die Steckdose
socks	die Socken
soda	das Soda
soft	weich
soft drink	das alkoholfreie Getränk
sole (of shoe)	die Sohle
(fish)	die Seezunge
soluble	löslich
some	einige
someone	irgendjemand
something	etwas

sometimes	manchmal
son	der Sohn
song	das Lied
soon	bald
as soon as possible	*so bald wie möglich*
sooner	früher
sore	weh
I have a sore throat	*ich habe Halsschmerzen*
sorry: I'm sorry!	*tut mir leid!*
sort	die Art
what sort of cheese?	*was für ein Käse?*
sound	der Ton
soup	die Suppe
sour	sauer
south	der Süden
souvenir	das Souvenir
space	der Raum
parking space	*der Parkplatz*
spade	der Spaten
spanner	der Schraubenschlüssel
spare parts	die Ersatzteile *(pl)*
spare wheel	der Ersatzreifen
sparkling	perlend
spark plugs	die Zündkerzen *(pl)*
speak	sprechen
special	besondere
speciality	die Spezialität
speed	die Geschwindigkeit
speed limit	die Geschwindigkeitsbegrenzung
speedometer	der Tachometer
spell: *how is it spelt?*	*wie buchstabiert man das?*
spend *(money)*	ausgeben
(time)	verbringen
spice	das Gewürz

spicy	würzig
spill	verschütten
spinach	der Spinat
spine *(backbone)*	das Rückgrat
spirits	die Spirituosen *(pl)*
spit	spucken
splinter	der Splitter
split	teilen
spoil	verderben
sponge	der Schwamm
spoon	der Löffel
sport	der Sport
spring *(season)*	der Frühling
square *(in town)*	der Platz
squash *(game, drink)*	das Squash
squeeze	quetschen
stain	der Fleck
stainless steel	rostfrei
stairs	die Treppe
stalls *(in theatre)*	das Parkett
stamp	die Briefmarke
stapler	die Heftmaschine
staples	die Heftklammern
star	der Stern
(film)	der Star
start *(begin)*	anfangen
starter	die Vorspeise
(in car)	der Anlasser
station	der Bahnhof
stationer's	die Schreibwarenhandlung
stay	bleiben
I'm staying at a hotel	*ich wohne in einem Hotel*
steak	das Steak
steel	der Stahl

steep	steil
steering	die Lenkung
steering wheel	das Steuer
step	der Schritt
(stair)	die Stufe
sterling (pounds)	das Pfund Sterling
stew	das Eintopfgericht
steward (on plane)	der Steward
stewardess	die Stewardeß
stick n	der Stock
stick vb (with glue)	kleben
sticking plaster	das Heftpflaster
sticky	klebrig
stiff	steif
still (yet)	noch
(motionless)	still
sting	der Stachel
stockings	die Strümpfe (pl)
stolen	gestohlen
stomach	der Magen
stomach upset	der verdorbene Magen
stone	der Stein
stop	halten
storm	der Sturm
straight on	geradeaus
strange (odd)	seltsam
stranger m/f	der/die Fremde
straw (for drinking)	der Strohhalm
strawberries	die Erdbeeren (pl)
stream	der Fluß
street	die Straße
street map	der Stadtplan
string	die Schnur
striped	gestreift

strong	stark
stuck: *it's stuck* (jammed)	es klemmt
student *m/f*	der/die Student(in)
stung	gestochen
stupid	dumm
style	der Stil
suburb	der Vorort
success	der Erfolg
suddenly	plötzlich
suede	das Wildleder
sugar	der Zucker
suit (man's)	der Anzug
(woman's)	das Kostüm
suitcase	der Koffer
summer	der Sommer
sun	die Sonne
sunbathe	sonnenbaden
sunburn	der Sonnenbrand
sunglasses	die Sonnenbrille
sunny	sonnig
sunshade	der Sonnenschirm
sunstroke	der Sonnenstich
suntan lotion	das Sonnenöl
supermarket	der Supermarkt
supper	das Abendessen
supplement	die Ergänzung
sure (definite)	bestimmt
surfboard	das Surfboard
surfing	das Surfen
surname	der Nachname
suspension (in car)	die Federung
surprise	die Überraschung
surrounded by	umgeben von

sweater	der Pullover
sweet	süß
sweetener	der Süßstoff
sweets	die Süßigkeiten
swim	schwimmen
swimming pool	das Schwimmbad
swimsuit	der Badeanzug
Swiss	schweizerisch
(person) m/f	der/die Schweizer(in)
switch	der Schalter
switch off *(light)*	ausschalten
(machine)	abschalten
(gas, water)	abstellen
switch on *(light, machine)*	einschalten
(gas, water)	anstellen
Switzerland	die Schweiz
synagogue	die Synagoge

table	der Tisch
tablecloth	die Tischdecke
tablespoon	der Eßlöffel
tablet	die Tablette
table wine	der Tafelwein
tailback	der Rückstau
take	nehmen
how long does it take?	*wie lange dauert es?*
talc	der Körperpuder
talk	sprechen
tall	groß
tampons	die Tampons
tape-recorder	das Tonbandgerät
tartar sauce	die Remouladensauce
taste *n*	der Geschmack

taste *vb*	probieren
tax	die Steuer
taxi	das Taxi
taxi rank	der Taxistand
tea	der Tee
tea bag	der Teebeutel
teach	unterrichten
teacher *m/f*	der/die Lehrer(in)
teapot	die Teekanne
teaspoon	der Teelöffel
teat	die Brustwarze
(on bottle)	der Sauger
teeshirt	das T-shirt
teeth	die Zähne *(pl)*
telegram	das Telegramm
telephone	das Telefon
telephone box	die Telefonzelle
telephone call	der Anruf
telephone directory	das Telefonbuch
television	das Fernsehen
television set	der Fernsehapparat
telex	das Telex
tell	erzählen
temperature	die Temperatur
I have a temperature	ich habe Fieber
temporary	provisorisch
tender *(meat)*	zart
tennis	das Tennis
tennis court	der Tennisplatz
tennis racket	der Tennisschläger
tent	das Zelt
tent peg	der Hering
terminal *(airport)*	das Terminal
terrace	die Terrasse

than: *better than this*	*besser als dies*
thank you	*danke*
thank you very much	*vielen Dank*
that	*das*
that one	*das dort*
theatre	*das Theater*
then	*dann*
there	*dort*
there is/there are	*es gibt*
thermometer	*das Thermometer*
these	*diese*
they	*sie see* **GRAMMAR**
thick	*dick*
thief *m/f*	*der/die Dieb(in)*
thigh	*der Oberschenkel*
thin	*dünn*
thing: *my things*	*meine Sachen*
think	*denken*
third	*dritte(r/s)*
thirsty	*durstig*
I'm thirsty	*ich habe Durst*
this	*dies*
this one	*das hier*
those	*jene*
thread	*der Faden*
throat	*die Kehle*
throat lozenges	*die Halspastillen*
through	*durch*
throw	*werfen*
thumb	*der Daumen*
thunder	*der Donner*
thunderstorm	*das Gewitter*
thyme	*der Thymian*
ticket	*die Karte*

ticket collector	der Schaffner
ticket office	der Fahrkartenschalter
tide	die Gezeiten *(pl)*
tie	die Krawatte
tights	die Strumpfhose
till *n*	die Kasse
till *prep*	bis
time	die Zeit
this time	*diesmal*
timetable	der Fahrplan
tin	die Dose
tinfoil	die Alufolie
tin-opener	der Dosenöffner
tip *(to waiter etc)*	das Trinkgeld
tipped *(cigarettes)*	Filter-
tired	müde
tissues	die Papiertaschentücher *(pl)*
to	zu
(with names of places)	nach
toast	der Toast
tobacco	der Tabak
tobacconist	die Tabakwarenhandlung
today	heute
together	zusammen
toilet	die Toilette
toilet paper	das Toilettenpapier
toll	die Maut
tomato	die Tomate
tomato juice	der Tomatensaft
tomorrow	morgen
tongue	die Zunge
tonic water	das Tonic
tonight	heute abend

too (also)	auch
it's too big	es ist zu groß
tooth	der Zahn
toothache: I have toothache	ich habe Zahnschmerzen
toothbrush	die Zahnbürste
toothpaste	die Zahnpasta
top adj : the top floor	das oberste Stockwerk
top n (of mountain)	der Gipfel
(lid)	der Deckel
(surface)	die Oberfläche
on top of...	oben auf
torch	die Taschenlampe
torn	zerrissen
total	die Endsumme
tough (meat)	zäh
tour	die Fahrt
tourist m/f	der/die Tourist(in)
tourist office	das Fremdenverkehrsbüro
tourist ticket	die Touristenkarte
tow (car, boot)	abschleppen
towel	das Handtuch
town	die Stadt
town centre	das Stadtzentrum
town plan	der Stadtplan
tow rope	das Abschleppseil
toy	das Spielzeug
traditional	traditionell
traffic	der Verkehr
trailer	der Anhänger
train	der Zug
training shoes	die Trainingsschuhe (pl)
tram	die Straßenbahn
translate	übersetzen

translation	die Übersetzung
travel	reisen
travel agent	das Reisebüro
traveller's cheques	die Reiseschecks
tray	das Tablett
treatment	die Behandlung
tree	der Baum
trim	nachschneiden
trip	der Ausflug
trouble	die Schwierigkeiten (pl)
trousers	die Hose
true	wahr
trunk	der Überseekoffer
trunks	die Badehose
try	versuchen
try on	anprobieren
T-shirt	das T-shirt
tuna	der Thunfisch
tunnel	der Tunnel
turkey	der Truthahn
turn (rotate)	drehen
turnip	die Rübe
turn off (light)	ausmachen
(tap)	zudrehen
turn on (light)	anmachen
(tap)	aufdrehen
tweezers	die Pinzette
twice	zweimal
twin-bedded room	das Zweibettzimmer
twins	die Zwillinge (pl)
typical	typisch
tyre	der Reifen
tyre pressure	der Reifendruck

umbrella	der Regenschirm
uncle	der Onkel
uncomfortable	unbequem
unconscious	bewußtlos
under	unter
underground	die U-Bahn
underpants	die Unterhose
underpass	die Unterführung
understand	verstehen
I don't understand	*ich verstehe nicht*
underwear	die Unterwäsche
unemployed	arbeitslos
unfasten	aufmachen
United States	die Vereinigten Staaten *(pl)*
university	die Universität
unleaded petrol	das bleifreie Benzin
unlock	aufschließen
unpack	auspacken
unscrew	aufschrauben
unusual	ungewöhnlich
up	auf
up there	*dort oben*
upset	betroffen
upside down	verkehrt herum
upstairs	oben
urgent	dringend
urine	der Urin
us	uns
USA	die USA *(pl)*
use	benützen
useful	nützlich
usual	gewöhnlich
usually	gewöhnlich
U-turn	die Wende

vacancies	Zimmer frei
vacuum cleaner	der Staubsauger
valid	gültig
valley	das Tal
valuable	wertvoll
valuables	die Wertsachen (pl)
van	der Lieferwagen
vase	die Vase
VAT	die Mehrwertsteuer (MWST)
veal	das Kalbfleisch
vegetables	das Gemüse
vegetarian	vegetarisch
vehicle	das Fahrzeug
venison	das Reh
ventilator	der Ventilator
vermouth	der Wermut
very	sehr
vest	das Unterhemd
via	über
video	das Video
video camera	die Videokamera
view	die Aussicht
villa	die Villa
village	das Dorf
vinegar	der Essig
vineyard	der Weinberg
visa	das Visum
visit	besuchen
vitamin	das Vitamin
vodka	der Wodka
voice	die Stimme
voltage	die Spannung
vote	wählen

waist	die Taille
wait for	warten auf
waiter	der Ober
waiting room	der Warteraum
waitress	die Kellnerin
wake up	aufwachen
Wales	Wales
walk *vb*	spazierengehen
walk: to go for a walk	*einen Spaziergang machen*
wallet	die Brieftasche
walnut	die Walnuß
want	wollen
warm	warm
warning triangle	das Warndreieck
wash	waschen
(to wash oneself)	sich waschen
washbasin	das Waschbecken
washing machine	die Waschmaschine
washing powder	das Waschpulver
washing-up liquid	das Spülmittel
wasp	die Wespe
waste bin	der Abfalleimer
watch *n*	die Armbanduhr
watch *vb*	zuschauen
watch strap	das Uhrarmband
water	das Wasser
waterfall	der Wasserfall
water heater	das Heißwassergerät
water melon	die Wassermelone
waterproof	wasserdicht
water-skiing	das Wasserskilaufen
water wings	die Schwimmflügel
wax	das Wachs

way (means)	die Weise
(direction)	der Weg
which is the way to...?	*wie kommt man zu/nach...?*
we	wir *see* GRAMMAR
weak	schwach
(coffee)	dünn
wear	tragen
weather	das Wetter
wedding	die Hochzeit
week	die Woche
weekday	der Werktag
weekend	das Wochenende
weekly rate	der Wochenpreis
weight	das Gewicht
welcome	willkommen
well	gut
he's not well	*ihm geht's nicht gut*
well done (steak)	durch
Welsh	walisisch
(person) m/f	der/die Waliser(in)
west	der Westen
wet	naß
wetsuit	der Taucheranzug
what	was
what is it?	*was ist das?*
wheel	das Rad
wheelchair	der Rollstuhl
when	wann
where	wo
which: which man?	*welcher Mann?*
which woman?	*welche Frau?*
which book?	*welches Buch?*
while conj	während
while n : in a while	bald
whipped (cream)	Schlag-

whisky	der Whisky
white	weiß
wing	der Flügel
(of car)	der Kotflügel
who: *who is it?*	*wer ist es?*
whole	vollständig
wholemeal bread	das Vollkornbrot
whose: *whose is it?*	*wem gehört es?*
why	warum
wide	weit
wife	die Frau
window	das Fenster
(of shop)	das Schaufenster
windscreen	die Windschutzscheibe
windsurfing	das Surfen
wine	der Wein
wine list	die Weinkarte
winter	der Winter
with	mit
without	ohne
woman	die Frau
wood (material)	das Holz
(forest)	der Wald
wool	die Wolle
word	das Wort
work (person)	arbeiten
(machine)	funktionieren
worried	besorgt
worse	schlimmer
worth: *it's worth £50*	*es ist £50 wert*
wrap (up)	einwickeln
write	schreiben
writing paper	das Briefpapier
wrong	falsch

X-ray	die Röntgenaufnahme
yacht	die Yacht
yawn	gähnen
year	das Jahr
yearly	jährlich
yellow	gelb
Yellow Pages	die Gelben Seiten
yes	ja
yes please	*(ja,) bitte*
yesterday	gestern
yet: *not yet*	noch nicht
yoghurt	der Joghurt
yolk *(of egg)*	das Eigelb
you *(polite sing. and pl.)*	Sie *see* **GRAMMAR**
(familiar)	du *(sing.)* ; *(pl.)* ihr
young	jung
youth hostel	die Jugendherberge
zero	null
zip	der Reißverschluß
zone	die Zone
zoo	der Zoo

Aal *m*	eel
Aalsuppe *f*	eel soup
ab	off ; from
ab 8 Uhr	from 8 o'clock
ab Mai	from May onward
abbestellen	to cancel
Abbildung *f*	illustration
abblenden	to dip (headlights)
Abblendlicht *nt*	dipped headlights
Abend *m*	evening
Abendessen *nt*	dinner
abends	in the evening(s)
aber	but
abfahren	to pull out ; to leave
Abfahrt *f*	departure
Abfahrtszeit *f*	departure time
Abfall *m*	rubbish
Abfertigungsschalter *m*	check-in desk
abfliegen	to take off (plane)
Abflug *m*	takeoff ; departure
Abflug Inland	domestic departures
Abflug Ausland	international departures
Abflughalle *f*	departure lounge
Abflugtafel *f*	departure board
Abflugzeit *f*	departure time
Abführmittel *nt*	laxative
abgelaufen	out-of-date
abheben	to withdraw (money)
abholen	to fetch ; to claim (baggage, etc.)
abholen lassen	to send for
ablaufen	to expire
Abreise *f*	departure
absagen	to cancel
abschalten	to switch off

abschicken	to dispatch
Abschleppdienst m	breakdown service
abschleppen	to tow
Abschleppseil nt	towrope
Abschleppstange f	towbar
Abschleppwagen m	breakdown van
Abschnitt m	counterfoil
Absender m	sender
Abstand m	distance ; interval (time)
Abstand halten!	keep your distance
abstellen	to turn off ; to park (car)
Abtei f	abbey
Abteil nt	compartment (on train)
Achse f	axle
achten auf	to pay attention to
Achtung f	attention ; danger
Ackersalat m	corn salad ; lamb's lettuce
Adresse f	address
adressieren	to address (letter)
Alarmanlage f	alarm
Alkohol m	liquor ; alcohol
alkoholfrei	non-alcoholic
alkoholisch	alcoholic (drink)
alle	all (plural) ; everybody ; everyone
alle zwei Tage	every other day
Allee f	avenue
allein	alone
allergisch gegen	allergic to
Allerheiligen nt	All Saints' Day
alle(r/s)	all (with singular noun)
alles	everything ; all (singular)
allgemein	general ; universal
Alpen pl	Alps

als	**than ; when** *(with past tense)*
alt	**old**
Altbier *nt*	**top-fermented dark beer**
Alter *nt*	**age** *(of person)*
ältere(r/s)	**older ; elder**
älteste(r/s)	**oldest ; eldest**
Alufolie *f*	**foil** *(for food)*
am	**at ; in ; on**
am Bahnhof	**at the station**
am Abend	**in the evening**
am Freitag	**on Friday**
Ampel *f*	**traffic light**
Amtszeichen *nt*	**dialling tone**
Amüsierviertel *nt*	**nightclub district**
an	**at ; on ; near**
Frankfurt an 1300	**arriving Frankfurt 13ôo**
an/aus	**on/off**
Ananas(se) *f*	**pineapple(s)**
anbieten	**to offer**
andere(r/s)	**other**
andere Richtungen	**other destinations**
anders	**differently ; else**
Änderung *f*	**change**
Anfang *m*	**start** *(beginning)*
anfangen	**to begin**
Anfänger(in) *m/f*	**beginner**
Anflug *m*	**approach** *(of plane)*
Anfrage *f*	**enquiry**
Angaben *pl*	**details ; directions** *(to a place)*
Angaben machen	**to make a statement**
angeben	**to give**
Angebot *nt*	**offer**
Angehörige(r) *m/f*	**relative**
Angeln *nt*	**fishing, angling**

Angelschein *m*	**fishing permit**
angenehm	**pleasant**
Angestellte(r) *m/f*	**employee**
Anhänger *m*	**trailer ; fan** (supporter)
Anis *m*	**aniseed**
Anker *m*	**anchor**
ankommen	**to arrive**
ankündigen	**to announce**
Ankunft(-künfte) *f*	**arrival(s)**
Anlage *f*	**park ; grounds ; facilities**
öffentliche Anlagen	**public park**
Anlegestelle *f*	**landing stage ; jetty**
anmachen	**to toss** (salad)
das Licht anmachen	**to put on the light**
Anmeldung *f*	**registration ; reception** (place)
Annahme *f*	**acceptance ; reception**
annehmen	**to assume ; to accept**
annullieren	**to cancel**
anprobieren	**to try on** (clothes)
Anruf *m*	**phone call**
Anrufbeantworter *m*	**telephone answering machine**
anrufen	**to telephone**
Anschluß *m*	**connection** (train, etc.)
Anschlußflug *m*	**connecting flight**
Anschrift *f*	**address**
Ansicht *f*	**view**
Ansichtskarte(n) *f*	**picture postcard(s)**
anstatt	**instead of**
ansteckend	**infectious**
Anteil *m*	**share** (part)
Antenne *f*	**aerial**
Antibiotikum *nt*	**antibiotic**
Antihistamin *nt*	**antihistamine**
Antiquariat *nt*	**second-hand bookshop**

Antiquität(en) f	antique(s)
Antwort f	answer ; reply
Anweisungen pl	instructions
Anzahl f	number
Anzahlung f	deposit
Anzeige f	advertisement ; report (to police)
Anzug(-züge) m	suit(s)
Anzünder m	lighter
Apfel (Äpfel) m	apple(s)
Apfelkorn m	apple brandy
Apfelkuchen m	apple cake
Apfelrösti pl	slices of fried apple and bread
Apfelsaft m	apple juice
Apfelsine(n) f	orange(s)
Apfelwein m	cider
Apotheke f	chemist's shop
Apparat m	appliance ; camera ; extension
Aprikose(n) f	apricot(s)
Arbeit f	labour ; employment ; work
arbeitslos	unemployed
Arm m	arm
Armbanduhr f	watch
Ärmelkanal m	Channel
Art f	type ; sort ; manner
Artikel m	article ; item
Artischocke f	globe artichoke
Artischockenherz nt	artichoke heart
Arznei f	medicine
Arzt (Ärztin) m/f	doctor
Aschenbecher m	ashtray
Aschermittwoch m	Ash Wednesday
atmen	to breathe
auch	also ; too ; as well

auf	onto ; on ; upon ; on top of
auf deutsch	in German
Aufenthalt *m*	stay ; visit
Aufenthaltsraum *m*	day room ; lounge
Auffahrt *f*	slip-road
Aufführung *f*	performance
aufgeben	to quit ; to check in *(baggage)*
aufhalten	to delay ; to hold up
sich aufhalten	to stay
Auflauf *m*	soufflé
auflegen	to hang up *(phone)*
aufmachen	to open *(shop, bank)*
sich aufmachen	to set off
aufschließen	to unlock
Aufschnitt *m*	cold meat ; assorted cheese
aufschreiben	to write down
Aufschub *m*	delay
Aufstieg *m*	ascent
Aufzug(n) *nt*	lift
Auge(n) *nt*	eye(s)
Augenblick *m*	moment ; instant ; point *(in time)*
einen Augenblick!	hold on! *(on phone)*
Auktion *f*	auction
aus	off *(machine, light)* ; from ; out of
Ausdruck *m*	expression ; print-out ; term *(word)*
Ausfahrt *f*	exit
Ausfahrt freihalten	keep clear
Ausfall *m*	failure *(mechanical)*
Ausflug(-flüge) *m*	trip(s)
Ausfuhr *f*	export(s)
ausführen	to export ; to carry out *(job)*
ausfüllen	to fill in
bitte nicht ausfüllen	please leave blank *(on form)*
Ausgabe *f*	issue *(of magazine)* ; issuing counter

German	English
Ausgaben *pl*	expenditure ; expenses
Ausgang *m*	exit ; gate *(at airport)*
ausgeben	to spend *(money)*
ausgeschaltet	off *(radio)*
ausgeschlossen	impossible
ausgestellt	issued *(passport)*
Auskunft *f*	information ; enquiries
Ausland *nt*	foreign countries ; abroad
aus dem Ausland	from overseas
Ausländer(in) *m/f*	foreigner
ausländisch	foreign
Auslandsgespräch *nt*	international call
auslassen	to leave out ; to miss out
auslaufen	to sail *(ship)*
ausmachen	to put out *(light)*
Ausnahme(n) *f*	exception(s)
ausrufen lassen	to page
Ausrüstung *f*	kit ; equipment
ausschalten	to switch off
Ausschank *m*	bar ; serving of drinks
Ausschlag *m*	rash
ausschließlich	exclusive of
Außenraum *m*	outer zone
Außenseite *f*	outside
Außenspiegel *m*	outside mirror
außer	except (for)
außer Betrieb	out of order
äußerlich	exterior
Aussicht *f*	prospect ; outlook ; view
Aussichtsterrasse *f*	observation deck
Aussichtsturm *m*	observation tower
Ausstattung *f*	equipment *(of car)*
aussteigen	to get out
Ausstellung *f*	show ; exhibition

Ausstellungsdatum *nt*	date of issue
Auster(n) *f*	oyster(s)
Ausverkauf *m*	sale
ausverkauft	sold out
Auswahl *f*	choice
Ausweis *m*	identity card ; pass *(permit)*
auszahlen	to pay
Auto(s) *nt*	car(s)
Autobahn *f*	motorway
Autobahngebühr *f*	toll
Autofähre *f*	car-ferry
Autokarte *f*	road map
Autokino *nt*	drive-in
Automat *m*	vending machine
Automat wechselt	change given
Automatikwagen *m*	automatic *(car)*
automatisch	automatic
Automobilklub *m*	automobile association
Autoreisezug *m*	motorail service/train
Autovermietung *f*	car hire
Autowäsche *f*	car wash
Babyflasche *f*	bottle
Babynahrung *f*	baby food
Babyraum *m*	mother and baby room
Bachforelle *f*	river trout
Backofen *m*	oven
Backpflaume(n) *f*	prune(s)
Bad *nt*	bath
Badeanstalt *f*	public swimming baths
Badeanzug *m*	swimsuit
Badehose *f*	swimming trunks

Bademütze f	bathing cap
baden	to bathe ; to swim
Baden verboten	no swimming
Badezimmer nt	bathroom
Bahn f	railway ; rink
per Bahn	by rail
Bahnhof m	station ; depot
Bahnlinie f	line (railway)
Bahnsteig m	platform
Bahnübergang m	level crossing
Bambussprossen pl	bamboo shoots
Banane(n) f	banana(s)
Band (Bänder) nt	ribbon(s) ; tape(s) (audio, video)
Band f	band (musical)
Bank f	bank (finance)
Bank f	bench (to sit on)
Bankkonto nt	bank account
Bar f	nightclub ; bar
bar bezahlen	to pay (in) cash
Bargeld nt	cash
Batterie f	battery
Bauarbeiten pl	roadworks
Bauernfrühstück nt	bacon and potato omelette
Bauernhof m	farm(yard)
Bauernsuppe f	cabbage soup with frankfurters
Baumwolle f	cotton (fabric)
Baustelle f	roadworks
beachten	to observe ; to obey
beantworten	to answer
Bedarfshaltestelle f	request stop
bedeckt	cloudy (weather)
Bedeutung f	meaning
bedienen	to serve ; to operate
sich bedienen	to help oneself

Bedienung *f*	service (charge)
Bedingung *f*	condition *(proviso)*
Beefsteak *nt*	steak
deutsches Beefsteak	hamburger ; beefburger
beenden	to end
Beere(n) *f*	berry (berries)
Begrenzung(en) *f*	limit(s)
begrüßen	to greet ; to welcome
behalten	to keep
Behandlung *f*	treatment
beheizt	heated
Behinderung *f*	obstruction
bei	near ; at ; on ; during ; care of
bei mir	at my house
beide	both
Beignet(s) *m*	fritter(s)
Beilage *f*	side-dish ; vegetables ; side-salad
Beispiel(e) *nt*	example(s)
zum Beispiel	for example
Beitrag *m*	contribution ; subscription *(to club)*
Bekenntnis *nt*	denomination
beladen	to load *(truck, ship)*
Belastung *f*	load
belegt	occupied ; no vacancies
Beleuchtung *f*	lighting
Belohnung *f*	reward
Bemerkung(en) *f*	comment(s) ; remark(s)
benachrichtigen	to inform
Benachrichtigung *f*	advice note
benutzen	to use
Benzin *nt*	petrol
Beratungsstelle *f*	advice centre
berechtigt zu	entitled to
Berechtigte(r) *m/f*	authorized person

German	English
Bereich m	area
im Bereich von	within the scope of
bereit	ready
Bereitschaftsdienst m	emergency service
Berg(e) m	mountain(s)
bergab	downhill
bergauf	uphill
Bergführer(in) m/f	mountain guide
Bergsteigen nt	mountaineering
bergsteigen gehen	to go mountaineering
Bergtour f	hillwalk ; climb
Bergwacht f	mountain rescue service
Bergwanderung f	hike in the mountains
Bericht(e) m	report(s) ; bulletin(s)
berichten	to report
Berliner m	doughnut
Berliner Weiße f	fizzy beer with fruit syrup added
Beruf m	profession, occupation
beruflich	professional
Beruhigungsmittel nt	tranquilliser
berühren	to handle ; to touch
beschädigen	to damage
Beschäftigung f	employment ; occupation
Bescheinigung f	certificate
Beschreibung f	description
besetzt	engaged (telephone)
Besichtigungen pl	sightseeing
Besitzer(in) m/f	owner
besondere(r/s)	particular ; special
besonders	especially ; extra
besser	better
Besserung(en) f	improvement(s)
gute Besserung	get well soon
bestätigen	to confirm

beste(r/s)	best
besteigen	to board (ship)
bestellen	to book ; to order
Bestellung f	order
bestimmt	definitely ; certainly
Bestimmungen pl	regulations
Bestimmungsort m	destination
Besucher(in) m/f	visitor
Besuchszeit f	visiting hours
Betrag m	amount
Betrag erhalten	payment received
betreffs	concerning
betreten	to enter
Betreten verboten	keep off
Betrieb m	business
außer Betrieb	out of order
betriebsbereit	operational
Bett(en) nt	bed(s)
Bettzeug nt	bedclothes
bewacht	guarded
Beweis m	proof
bewölkt	cloudy (weather)
bezahlen	to pay (for) ; to settle (bill)
bezahlt	paid
Bezahlung f	payment
Bibliothek f	library
Bienenstich m	bee sting
Bier(e) nt	beer(s)
Bier vom Faß	draught beer
Biergarten m	beer garden
Bierschinken m	ham sausage
Bierstengel m	bread stick
Bierstube f	pub which specializes in beer
Biersuppe f	beer soup

Bierwurst f	slightly smoked pork sausage
bieten	to offer
Bild(er) nt	picture(s)
Bildschirm m	screen (TV, computer, etc.)
billig	cheap ; inexpensive
Birne(n) f	pear(s) ; lightbulb(s)
bis	until
bis jetzt	up till now
bis zu 6	up to 6
bis bald	see you soon
Bismarckhering m	soused herring with onions
bißchen: ein bißchen	a little ; a bit of
bitte	please
bitte?	pardon? ; (I beg your) pardon?
Bitte f	request
bitter	bitter
bittere Schokolade	plain chocolate
Blatt (Blätter) nt	sheet(s) (of paper) ; leaf (leaves)
Blattsalat m	green salad
blau	blue ; au bleu (fish)
Blaukraut nt	red cabbage
Blauschimmelkäse m	blue cheese
bleiben	to remain ; to stay
bleichen	to bleach
bleifrei	unleaded ; lead-free
Blockschrift f	block letters
Blumenkohl m	cauliflower
Blut nt	blood
Blutdruck m	blood pressure
Blutgruppe f	blood group
Blutprobe f	blood test
Blutvergiftung f	blood poisoning
Blutwurst f	blood sausage ; black pudding
Bockbier nt	bock (beer) (strong beer)

Bocksbeutel *m*	dry (white) wine from Franconia
Bockwurst *f*	boiled sausage
Bohnen *pl*	beans
grüne Bohnen	French beans
Bohnensuppe *f*	thick bean soup
Boiler *m*	immersion heater
Bonbon *nt*	sweet
Boot *nt*	boat
Bootsverleih *m*	boat hire
Bordkarte *f*	boarding pass
Böschung *f*	embankment
botanischer Garten *m*	botanical gardens
Botschaft *f*	embassy
Bouillon *f*	clear soup
Bowle *f*	punch *(drink)*
Brat-	fried ; roast
Bratapfel *m*	baked apple
braten	to fry ; to roast
Bratensaft *m*	gravy
Brathähnchen *nt*	roast chicken
Brathering *m*	fried herring *(eaten cold)*
Bratkartoffeln *pl*	fried or sauté potatoes
Bratspieß *m*	spit *(for roasting)*
Bratwurst *f*	sausage
Brauerei *f*	brewery
Bräune *f*	tan *(on skin)*
Brechreiz *m*	nausea
breit	wide
Bremse(n) *f*	brake(s)
bremsen	to brake
brennen	to burn
Brezel *f*	pretzel
Brief *m*	letter *(message)*

Briefkasten *m*	letterbox ; postbox
Briefmarke(n) *f*	stamp(s)
Briefpapier *nt*	notepaper
britisch	British
Brombeere(n) *f*	blackberry (-berries)
Brot *nt*	bread ; loaf
Brötchen *nt*	bread roll
Brücke *f*	bridge
Bruder (Brüder) *m*	brother(s)
Brühe *f*	stock *(for soup, etc.)*
Brunnen *m*	well *(for water)* ; fountain
buchen	to book
Buchhandlung *f*	bookshop
Büchsen-	canned
Büchsenöffner *m*	can-opener
Buchstabe *m*	letter *(of alphabet)*
in Buchstaben	in words
Buchung *f*	booking
Bügel *m*	coat hanger
Bügel drücken!	press down!
bügelfrei	drip-dry
Bundes-	federal
Bundesbahn	federal railway
Bundesrepublik Deutschland *f*	Germany
Bündnerfleisch *nt*	cured dried beef, thinly sliced
bunt	coloured
buntes Glasfenster	stained glass window
Burg *f*	castle *(medieval)*
bürgerlich	middle-class
Bürgermeister(in) *m/f*	mayor(-ess)
Büro *nt*	agency ; office
Bus(se) *m*	bus(es) ; coach(es)
Bushaltestelle *f*	bus stop

Buslinie f	bus route
Büstenhalter m	bra
Busverbindung f	bus service
Butangas nt	Calor gas®
Butterkäse m	(full fat) cheese
Buttermilch f	buttermilk
Campingführer m	camping guide(book)
Champignon(s) m	mushroom(s)
Chinakohl m	Chinese cabbage
Chinarestaurant nt	Chinese restaurant
Chips pl	crisps ; chips (for gambling)
Christi Himmelfahrt f	Ascension Day (public holiday)
Cola f	Coke®
Cremespeise f	mousse
da	there
nicht da	out (not at home)
Dach nt	roof
daheim	at home
Dame f	lady
Damen	Ladies (toilet)
Damenbinde(n) f	sanitary towel(s)
dämpfen	to steam (food)
Dampfnudeln pl	sweet yeast dumplings
danke	thank you
Darmgrippe f	gastric flu
das	the ; that ; this ; which
das heißt ...	that is (to say)
Dattel(n) f	date(s) (fruit)
Datum nt	date (day)
Dauer f	duration

Decke f	blanket ; ceiling
Deckel m	top ; lid
Denkmal(-mäler) nt	monument(s)
der	the ; who(m)
desinfizieren	to disinfect
deutsch	German
Deutschland nt	Germany
Devisen pl	foreign currency
Dia(s) nt	slide(s)
Diabetiker(in) m/f	diabetic
dick	thick ; fat (person)
Dickmilch f	soured milk
die	the ; who(m)
Diebstahl m	theft
Dienst m	service
im Dienst	on duty
Dienstag m	Tuesday
dienstbereit	open (pharmacy) ; on duty (doctor)
Dienstzeit f	office hours
Diesel(kraftstoff) m	diesel oil
Dieselöl nt	diesel fuel
diese(r/s)	this (one)
Ding(e) nt	thing(s)
direkt	direct
Direktflug(-flüge) m	direct flight(s)
Dolmetscher(in) m/f	interpreter
Dom m	cathedral
Donnerstag m	Thursday
Doppelbett nt	double bed
doppelt	double
Doppelzimmer nt	double room
Dorf (Dörfer) nt	village(s)
Dorsch m	Atlantic cod

dort	**there**
Dose f	**box ; tin**
Dosenöffner m	**tin-opener**
Draht m	**wire**
Drahtseilbahn f	**cable railway**
draußen	**outdoors**
drehen	**to turn ; to twist**
Dreibettabteil nt	**three-berth compartment**
Dreieck nt	**triangle**
Dreikönigstag m	**Epiphany** (public holiday)
dringend	**urgent**
drinnen	**inside**
Droge f	**drug**
Drogerie f	**chemist's** (not for prescriptions)
drücken	**to press ; to push ; to print**
Drucksache f	**printed matter**
Druckschrift f	**block letters**
du	**you** (familiar form)
dumm	**stupid**
Düne(n) f	**dune(s)**
dunkel	**dark**
dünn	**thin ; weak** (tea)
durch	**through ; done** (meat)
Durchfall m	**diarrhoea**
Durchgang m	**way ; passage**
Durchgangsverkehr m	**through traffic**
durchgebraten	**well-done** (steak)
durchgehend	**through** (train)
Durchsage f	**announcement**
durchwählen	**to dial direct**
dürfen	**to be allowed**
Dusche f	**shower**
Dutzend nt	**dozen**

Ebbe *f*	low tide
echt	real ; genuine
Ecke *f*	corner *(of streets)*
Edamer *m*	German version of Edam
Edelstein *m*	jewel ; gem
ehemalig	ex-
Ei(er) *nt*	egg(s)
Eiersalat *m*	egg mayonnaise salad
Eigentum *nt*	property
Eigentümer(in) *m/f*	owner
Eil-	urgent
Eilbrief *m*	express letter
Eilzustellung *f*	special delivery
ein	a ; one
ein/aus	on/off
ein(e)	a ; an
Einbahnstraße *f*	one-way street
einchecken	to check in
einfach	simple
einfache Fahrkarte	single ticket
Einfuhr *f*	import
einführen	to insert ; to import
Eingang *m*	entrance ; gate
ein(geschaltet)	on *(machine)*
eingeschlossen	included *(in price)*
einige(r/s)	some ; a few
einkaufen	to shop
Einkaufszentrum *nt*	shopping centre
Einladung *f*	invitation
einlösen	to cash *(cheque)*
einordnen	to get in lane
Einrichtungen *pl*	facilities
eins	one

einschalten	**to switch on** *(light, TV)*
einschieben	**to insert**
einschließlich	**including**
Einschreiben *nt*	**certified mail**
per Einschreiben	**by recorded delivery**
einsteigen	**to board** *(train, bus)*
einstellen	**to adjust ; to appoint ; to stop**
Eintopf *m*	**stew**
Eintritt *m*	**entry ; admission** *(fee)*
Eintritt frei	**admission free**
Eintrittsgeld *nt*	**entrance fee**
Eintrittskarte(n) *f*	**ticket(s)**
Einwegmiete *f*	**one-way rental**
einwerfen	**to post ; to insert**
Einwurf *m*	**slot ; slit**
Einwurf 2 Mark	**insert 2 marks**
Einzahlung *f*	**deposit**
Einzelbett *nt*	**single bed**
Einzelfahrschein *m*	**single ticket**
einzeln	**single ; individual**
Einzelreisende(r) *m/f*	**person travelling alone**
Einzelzimmer *nt*	**single room**
Eis *nt*	**ice cream ; ice**
Eis am Stiel	**ice lolly**
Eisbahn *f*	**skating rink**
Eisbecher *m*	**knickerbocker glory**
Eisenbahn *f*	**railway**
Eisenwaren *pl*	**hardware**
Eiskaffee *m*	**iced coffee**
Eiswürfel *m*	**ice cube**
Elastikbinde *f*	**elastic bandage**
elektrisch	**electric(al)**
Elektrizität *f*	**electricity**
Eltern *pl*	**parents**

Empfang m	welcome ; reception
empfangen	to receive (guest)
Empfangsschein m	receipt
empfehlen	to recommend
Ende nt	bottom (of page, list) ; end
Endstation f	terminal
eng	narrow ; tight (clothes)
englisch	English ; rare (steak)
auf englisch	in English
Ente f	duck
entfernt	distant
2 Kilometer entfernt	2 kilometres away
Entfernung f	distance
Enthaarungscreme f	depilatory cream
enthalten	to contain
entrahmte Milch f	skimmed milk
Entschuldigung f	pardon ; excuse me
entweder ... oder	either ... or ...
entwickeln	to develop (photo)
Entzündung f	inflammation
er	he ; it
Erbsen pl	peas
Erdäpfelknödel pl	potato dumplings
Erdäpfelnudeln pl	fried potato balls in breadcrumbs
Erdbeere(n) f	strawberry(-berries)
Erdgeschoß nt	ground floor
Erdnuß(-nüsse) f	peanut(s)
Erfrischungen pl	refreshments
erhalten	to receive (letter)
erhältlich	obtainable ; available
Erkältung f	cold (illness)
Erklärung f	explanation
erlauben	to permit (something)
Ermäßigung f	reduction

Ersatz *m*	substitute ; replacement
Ersatzrad *nt*	spare wheel
ersetzen	to replace (substitute)
erste(r/s)	first
Erste Hilfe	first aid
Erwachsene(r) *m/f*	adult
es	it
eßbar	edible
essen	to eat
Essen *nt*	food ; meal
Essig *m*	vinegar
Etage *f*	floor ; storey
Etagenbetten *pl*	bunk beds
etwas	something
europäisch	European
Euroscheck *m*	Eurocheque
Exemplar *nt*	copy (of book, etc.)
Fabrik *f*	works ; factory
Fahrbahn *f*	carriageway
Fähre *f*	ferry
fahren	to drive ; to go
Fahrer(in) *m/f*	chauffeur ; driver (of car)
Fahrgast *m*	passenger
Fahrkarte(n) *f*	ticket(s)
Fahrkartenschalter *m*	ticket office
Fahrplan *m*	timetable (for trains, etc.)
Fahrplanhinweise *pl*	travel information
Fahrpreis(e) *m*	fare(s)
Fahrrad(-räder) *nt*	bicycle(s)
Fahrschein(e) *m*	ticket(s)
Fahrscheinentwerter *m*	ticket stamping machine

Fahrspur(en) f	lane(s)
Fahrstuhl m	lift
Fahrt f	journey ; drive ; ride *(in vehicle)*
gute Fahrt!	safe journey!
Fahrzeug nt	vehicle
Fall m	instance
im Falle von	in case of
fällig	due *(owing)*
falsch	false *(name, etc.)* ; wrong
Familie f	family
Familienname m	surname
Familienstand m	marital status
Farbe f	colour ; paint ; suit *(cards)*
Farbfilm m	colour film
farbig	coloured
Farbstoff m	dye
Fasan m	pheasant
Fasching m	carnival
Faß nt	barrel
vom Faß	on tap ; on draught
Faßbier nt	draught beer
Fastnachtsdienstag m	Shrove Tuesday
Feder f	spring *(coil)* ; feather
Federball m	badminton
fehlen	to be missing
Fehler m	fault ; mistake
feiern	to celebrate
Feiertag m	holiday
Feige(n) f	fig(s)
Feinkostgeschäft nt	delicatessen
Feldsalat m	corn salad ; lamb's lettuce
Fenchel m	fennel
Fenster nt	window
Fensterplatz m	seat by the window

Ferien *pl*	holiday(s)
Ferienhaus *nt*	(holiday) chalet
Ferienwohnung *f*	holiday flat
Fern-	long-distance
Fernamt *nt*	telephone exchange
Fernglas *nt*	binoculars
Fernlicht *nt*	full beam *(headlights)*
Fernsehen *nt*	television
Fernsprecher *m*	(public) telephone
fertig	ready ; finished
Fest *nt*	celebration ; party
Fett *nt*	fat ; grease
fettarm	low-fat
Feuer *nt*	fire
feuergefährlich	inflammable
Feuerlöscher *m*	fire extinguisher
Feuertreppe *f*	fire escape
Feuerwehr *f*	fire brigade
Feuerwerk *nt*	fireworks
Feuerzeug *nt*	cigarette lighter
Fieber *nt*	fever
Filet *nt*	sirloin ; fillet *(of meat, fish)*
Filiale *f*	branch *(of store, bank, etc.)*
Fisch *m*	fish
Fischauflauf *m*	fish pudding *(Austria)*
Fischstäbchen *pl*	fish fingers
Fischsuppe *f*	fish soup
flambiert	flambé
Flamme *f*	flame
Flasche *f*	bottle
Flaschenöffner *m*	bottle opener
Fleckenmittel *nt*	stain-remover
Fleisch *nt*	meat ; flesh

Fleischbrühe f	bouillon ; stock
Fleischerei f	butcher's (shop)
Fleischkäse m	meatloaf
Fleischklößchen nt	meatball
Flickzeug nt	puncture repair kit
Fliege f	bow tie ; fly
fliegen	to fly
Flohmarkt m	flea market
Flug (Flüge) m	flight(s)
Fluggast m	passenger
Fluggesellschaft f	airline
Flughafen m	airport
Flughafenbus m	airport bus
Flugnummer f	flight number
Flugplan m	flight schedule
Flugplanauskunft f	flight information
Flugschein(e) m	plane ticket(s)
Flugsteig m	gate
Flugstrecke f	route ; flying distance
Flugticket(s) nt	plane ticket(s)
Flugzeug nt	plane, aircraft
Fluß (Flüsse) m	river(s)
Flüssigkeit f	liquid
Flußkrebs m	crawfish ; crayfish
Flut f	flood ; tide
folgen	to follow
folgend	following
Fönen nt	blow-dry
Forelle f	trout
Forelle Steiermark	trout with bacon in white sauce
Forelle blau	steamed trout
Forelle Müllerin	trout fried in batter with almonds
Forellenfilet nt	fillet of smoked trout
Form f	shape ; form

Formular *nt*	**form** (document)
Foto *nt*	photo
Fotoapparat *m*	camera
Fotogeschäft *nt*	photographic shop
fotokopieren	to photocopy
Fracht *f*	cargo ; freight
Frage *f*	question
fragen	to ask
Frankenwein *m*	wine from Bavaria (fairly dry)
frankieren	to stamp (letter)
Frankreich *nt*	France
Franzose *m*	Frenchman
Französin *f*	Frenchwoman
französisch	French
Frau *f*	Mrs ; Ms ; woman ; wife
Fräulein *nt*	Miss
frei	free ; clear ; vacant
im Freien	outdoor ; open-air
Freibad *nt*	open-air swimming pool
Freigepäck *nt*	baggage allowance
freimachen	to stamp
Freizeichen *nt*	ringing tone
Freizeit *f*	spare time ; leisure
fremd	foreign ; strange (unknown)
Fremde(r) *m/f*	stranger
Fremdenführer(in) *m/f*	courier (tour guide)
Fremdenverkehr *m*	tourism
Freund *m*	friend ; boyfriend
Freundin *f*	friend ; girlfriend
Friedhof *m*	cemetery
frisch	fresh ; wet (paint)
Frischhaltefolie *f*	cling film
Frischkäse *m*	cream cheese

Friseur(-euse) m/f	hairdresser
Frostschutzmittel nt	antifreeze
Früchte pl	fruit
Fruchtsaft m	fruit juice
früh	early
Frühling m	spring (season)
Frühlingsrolle(n) f	spring or pancake roll(s)
Frühlingssuppe f	vegetable soup with noodles
Frühstück nt	breakfast
Frühstücksbuffet nt	breakfast buffet
Führer(in) m/f	guide
Führerschein m	driving licence
Führung f	guided tour
Fundbüro nt	lost property office
Fundsachen pl	lost property
für	for
Benzin für DM50	DM50 worth of petrol
Fuß (Füße) m	foot (feet)
zu Fuß gehen	to walk
Fußball m	football ; soccer
Fußgänger(in) m/f	pedestrian
Fußgängerüberweg m	pedestrian crossing
Fußweg m	footpath
Gang m	course (of meal) ; passage (in house)
Gangschaltung f	gears
Gans f	goose
Gänseleberpastete f	pâté de foie gras
ganz	whole ; quite
ganztägig	full-time
gar	done (vegetables)
Garantie f	guarantee ; warrant(y)
Garderobe f	cloakroom ; wardrobe

German	English
Garnele(n) f	prawn(s)
Gartenlokal nt	garden café
Gasse f	alley ; lane (in town)
Gast m	guest
nur für Gäste	patrons only
Gästezimmer nt	guest-room
Gasthaus nt	inn
Gasthof m	inn
Gaststätte f	restaurant
Gaststube f	lounge
Gebäck nt	pastry (cake)
gebeizt	cured ; marinated
geben	to give
Gebiet nt	region ; area
Gebiß nt	dentures
geboren	born
geborene Schnorr	née Schnorr
gebraten	fried
gebratene Ente	roast duck
Gebrauch m	use
gebrauchen	to use
Gebraucht-	used (car, etc.)
Gebühr f	fee
gebührenpflichtig	subject to a charge
Geburtsdatum nt	date of birth
Geburtsort m	place of birth
Geburtstag m	birthday
Geburtsurkunde f	birth certificate
gedünstet	steamed
Gefahr f	danger
gefährlich	dangerous
Gefälle nt	gradient
Geflügel nt	poultry
gefroren	frozen (food)

gefüllt	stuffed
gegen	versus ; against ; toward(s)
Gegend f	district ; region
gegenüber	opposite ; facing
Gehacktes nt	mince
gehen	to go ; to walk
wie geht es Ihnen?	how are you?
gelb	yellow
Geld nt	money
Geld einwerfen	insert money
Geldautomat m	cash dispenser
Geldrückgabe f	coin return
Geldschein m	banknote
Geldstrafe f	fine
Geldstück nt	coin
Geltungsdauer f	period of validity
gemischt	mixed ; assorted
Gemüse nt	vegetables
genau	accurate ; precise ; exact(ly)
Genehmigung f	approval ; permit
Genuß m	enjoyment
geöffnet	open
Gepäck nt	luggage
Gepäckaufbewahrung f	left-luggage office
Gepäckausgabe f	baggage reclaim
Gepäckermittlung f	luggage desk (for queries)
Gepäcknetz nt	luggage rack (in train)
Gepäckschließfach nt	left-luggage locker
Gepäckträger m	luggage rack (on car) ; porter
Gepäckversicherung f	luggage insurance
geradeaus	straight ahead
Gerät nt	appliance ; gadget
geräuchert	smoked

209

Gericht *nt*	court *(law)* ; dish *(food)*
geröstet	sauté ; fried ; toasted
Geruch *m*	smell
Geschäft(e) *nt*	shop(s)
Geschäftsstunden *pl*	business hours
Geschenk(e) *nt*	gift(s)
geschieden	divorced
Geschirrspülmittel *nt*	washing-up liquid
Geschlecht *nt*	gender ; sex
geschlossen	closed
Geschmack *m*	taste ; flavour
geschmort	braised
Geschwindigkeit *f*	speed
gesetzlich	legal
gesetzlicher Feiertag	public holiday
gesperrt	closed
Gespräch *nt*	talk ; (telephone) call
gestattet	permitted
gestern	yesterday
Gesundheit *f*	health
Getränk(e) *nt*	drink(s)
Getränkekarte *f*	list of beverages ; wine list
Getriebe *nt*	gearbox
Gewehr *nt*	gun
Gewicht *nt*	weight
Gewürz *nt*	spice ; seasoning
Gewürzgurke(n) *f*	gherkin(s)
Gezeiten *pl*	tide
gibt es...?	is there...? ; are there...?
Gift *nt*	poison
giftig	poisonous
Gitarre *f*	guitar
Gitziprägel *nt*	baked rabbit in batter *(Switzerland)*

Glas *nt*	glass ; lens *(of glasses)* ; jar
Glatteisgefahr *f*	danger of black ice
Glocke *f*	bell
Glück *nt*	happiness ; luck
Glühbirne *f*	light bulb
Golfplatz *m*	golf course
Golfschläger *m*	golf club
Gott *m*	God
Gottesdienst *m*	church service
Grad *nt*	degree *(of heat, cold)*
grau	grey
Grenze *f*	frontier ; border
Griff *m*	handle ; knob
Grillteller *m*	mixed grill
Grippe *f*	flu
groß	tall ; great ; big ; wide *(range)*
Großbritannien *nt*	Great Britain
Großbuchstabe(n) *m*	capital letter(s)
Größe *f*	size ; height
grün	green ; fresh *(fish)*
Grünanlage *f*	park
Gründonnerstag *m*	Maundy Thursday
Gruß *m*	greeting
Gulasch *nt*	goulash
gültig	valid
Gummi *m*	rubber ; elastic
günstig	convenient
Gurke(n) *f*	cucumber(s) ; gherkin(s)
Gürtel *m*	belt
gut	good ; well ; all right *(yes)*
guten Appetit	enjoy your meal
alles Gute	all the best ; with best wishes
Güter *pl*	goods
Gutschein *m*	voucher ; coupon

Haar *nt*	hair
haben	to have *see* GRAMMAR
Hackfleisch *nt*	mince
Hacksteak *nt*	hamburger
Hafen *m*	harbour ; port
Haftung *f*	liability
Hagebuttentee *m*	rosehip tea
Hahn *m*	tap *(for water)* ; cockerel
Hähnchen *nt*	chicken
halb	half
zum halben Preis	half-price
halbdurch	medium *(steak)*
Halbpension *f*	half board
Hälfte *f*	half
Hals *m*	neck ; throat
Halsschmerzen *pl*	sore throat
halten	to hold ; to stop
Haltestelle *f*	bus stop
Hammelfleisch *nt*	mutton
Handel *m*	trade ; commerce
handgearbeitet	handmade
handgemacht	handmade
Handgepäck *nt*	hand-luggage
Handschuhe *pl*	gloves
Handtasche *f*	handbag
Handtuch *nt*	towel
Handwerker(in) *m/f*	craftsman(-woman)
Hase *m*	hare
Haselnuß(-nüsse) *f*	hazelnut(s)
häufig	frequent ; common
Haupt-	major ; main
Hauptgericht(e) *nt*	main course(s)
Hauptstadt *f*	capital *(city)*

Hauptverkehrszeit f	peak hours
Haus nt	house ; home
zu Hause	at home
Haushaltswaren pl	household goods
Hauswein m	house wine
Haut f	hide (leather) ; skin
Hecht m	pike
Hefe f	yeast
Heftpflaster nt	sticking plaster
Heilbutt m	halibut
Heiligabend m	Christmas Eve
Heim nt	home (institution) ; hostel
heiß	hot
heißen	to be called
wie heißen Sie?	what is your name?
Heißwassergerät nt	water heater
Heizgerät nt	heater
Heizkörper m	radiator
Heizung f	heating
helfen	to help
hell	light (pale) ; bright
Helm m	helmet
Hemd(en) nt	shirt(s)
Herbst m	autumn
herein	in ; come in
Hering m	herring ; peg
Heringstopf m	pickled herrings in soured cream
Herr m	gentleman ; master ; Mr
Herren	Gents (toilet)
Herrentoilette f	gents' toilet
Herz nt	heart
Herzmuschel(n) f	cockle(s)
Heuschnupfen m	hay fever
heute	today

heute abend	tonight
hier	here
hiesig	local
Hilfe *f*	help
Himbeere(n) *f*	raspberry(-berries)
Himbeergeist *m*	raspberry brandy
hin	there
hinten	behind
Hin- und Rückfahrt *f*	round trip
Hinweis *m*	notice
Hirsch *m*	venison
hoch	high
Hochsaison *f*	high season
Höhe *f*	altitude ; height *(of object)*
höher	higher
höher stellen	to turn up *(heat, volume)*
Höhle *f*	cave
holländisch	Dutch
Holz *nt*	wood *(material)*
Honig *m*	honey
hören	to hear
Hörer *m*	receiver *(phone)*
Hörgerät *nt*	hearing aid
Hörnchen *nt*	croissant
Hose *f*	trousers
Hotel garni *nt*	bed and breakfast hotel
Hubschrauber *m*	helicopter
Huhn *nt*	chicken
Hummer *m*	lobster
Hund *m*	dog
Hupe *f*	horn *(of car)*
Husten *m*	cough
Hut *m*	hat

ich	I
Idiotenhügel *m*	nursery slope
Imbiß *m*	snack
Imbißstube *f*	snack bar
immer	always
inbegriffen	included
Infektion *f*	infection
Ingwer *m*	ginger
Inhalt *m*	contents
inklusive	inclusive
Inland *nt*	inland
Inlandsgespräch(e) *nt*	national call(s)
innen	inside
Innenstadt *f*	city centre
innerlich	for internal use (*medicine*)
Insel *f*	island
irgendwo	somewhere
Irrtum *m*	mistake
Italien *nt*	Italy
italienisch	Italian
ja	yes
Jacke *f*	jacket ; cardigan
Jägerschnitzel *nt*	pork escalope with mushrooms
Jahr *nt*	year
Jahreszeit *f*	season
Jahrgang *m*	vintage
Jahrhundert *nt*	century
jährlich	annual ; yearly
Jahrmarkt *m*	fair
Jakobsmuschel(n) *f*	scallop(s)
Januar *m*	January

jede(r/s)	each ; every
jemand	somebody ; someone
jetzt	now
Jod *nt*	iodine
Joghurt *m or nt*	yoghurt
Johannisbeere(n) *f*	currant(s)
Jugend *f*	youth *(period)*
Jugendherberge *f*	youth hostel
Jugendliche(r) *m /f*	teenager
Jugoslawien *nt*	Yugoslavia
Juli *m*	July
jung	young
Junge *m*	boy
Junggeselle *m*	bachelor
Juni *m*	June
Jura Omelette *f*	bacon, potato and onion omelette
Kabel *nt*	cable ; lead *(electrical)*
Kabeljau *m*	cod
Kaffee *m*	coffee
Kaffeemaschine *f*	percolator
Kai *m*	quayside
Kakao *m*	cocoa
Kalb *nt*	calf
Kalbfleisch *nt*	veal
Kalbsbries *nt*	calf's sweetbread
Kalbsleber *f*	calf's liver
Kalbsschnitzel *nt*	veal escalope
kalt	cold
KaltererSee *m*	light red wine
Kamillentee *m*	camomile tea
Kamm *m*	comb ; ridge

kandiert	glacé
Kaninchen *nt*	rabbit
Kanister *m*	(petrol) can
Kanu *nt*	canoe
Kapelle *f*	chapel ; orchestra
Kapern *pl*	capers
kaputt	broken ; out of order
Karaffe *f*	decanter ; carafe
Karfreitag *m*	Good Friday
Karotten *pl*	carrots
Karpfen *m*	carp
Karte *f*	card ; ticket ; chart ; menu
Kartentelefon *nt*	cardphone
Kartoffel(n) *f*	potato(es)
Kartoffelbrei *m*	mashed potatoes
Kartoffelklöße *pl*	potato dumplings
Kartoffelpüree *nt*	mashed potatoes
Kartoffelsalat *m*	potato salad
Käse *m*	cheese
Käsekuchen *m*	cheesecake
Käseplatte *f*	(plate of) assorted cheeses
Kasse *f*	cash desk ; box office
Kassette *f*	cassette ; cartridge
Kastanie *f*	chestnut
kaufen	to buy
Kaufhaus *nt*	department store
Kaugummi *m*	chewing gum
Kaution *f*	deposit
kein(e)	no ; not a(n)
Keks(e) *m*	biscuit(s) *(sweet)*
Keller *m*	cellar
Kellner(in) *m/f*	waiter(-ress) ; steward *(at club)*
Keramik *f*	pottery

Kette f	chain
Kilometer m	kilometre
Kind(er) nt	child(ren)
Kinderbett nt	cot
Kinderteller m	child's helping
Kino nt	cinema
Kirche f	church
Kirsche(n) f	cherry (cherries)
Klarer m	schnapps
Klasse f	class ; grade
Klebstoff m	glue
Kleider pl	clothes
Kleiderbügel m	coat hanger
klein	short (person) ; small
Kleingeld nt	change (money)
Klettern	rock-climbing
Klimaanlage f	air-conditioning
klimatisiert	air-conditioned
Klingel f	bell
Kloß m	dumpling
Kloster nt	monastery ; convent
Knoblauch m	garlic
Knochen m	bone
Knödel m	dumpling
Knopf m	button ; knob (on radio, etc.)
kochen	to boil ; to cook
Kocher m	cooker ; stove
koffeinfrei	decaffeinated
Koffer m	suitcase
Kofferanhänger m	luggage tag
Kofferraum m	boot (of car)
Kohl m	cabbage
Kohlrübe f	swede

Koje f	berth (in ship) ; bunk
Kokosnuß f	coconut
Kölnischwasser nt	cologne
Kölsch nt	strong lager type beer
kommen	to come
Kommißbrot nt	rye bread
Komödie f	comedy
Kondensmilch f	condensed milk
Konditorei f	cake shop ; café
Kondom nt	condom
Konfektions-	ready-made (clothes)
Konfitüre f	jam
König m	king
Königin f	queen
Königinpastete f	vol-au-vent
königlich	royal
können	to be able ; to know
Konsulat nt	consulate
Kontaktlinsen pl	contact lenses
Kontrolle f	check ; control
kontrollieren	to check (ticket, etc.)
Kontzert nt	concert
Konzertsaal m	concert hall
Kopfhörer m	headphones
Kopfkissen nt	pillow
Kopfsalat m	lettuce
Kopfschmerzen pl	headache
Korken m	cork (of bottle)
Korkenzieher m	corkscrew
Körper m	body
Kosmetiktücher pl	paper tissues
kosten	to cost
kostenlos	free (costing nothing)

Kotelett nt	cutlet
Krabben pl	shrimps
Krabbencocktail m	prawn cocktail
Kräcker m	biscuit (savoury) ; cracker
Kraftstoff m	fuel
krank	ill ; sick
Krankenhaus nt	hospital
Krankenwagen m	ambulance
Kräuter pl	herbs
Krautsalat m	coleslaw
Krawatte f	tie
Krebs m	crab (animal) ; cancer (illness)
Kreditkarte f	credit card
Kreisverkehr m	roundabout
Kresse f	watercress ; cress
Kreuz nt	cross
Kreuzfahrt f	cruise
Kreuzung f	junction ; crossroads
Krevetten pl	shrimps
Krieg m	war
Küche f	kitchen ; cooking
Kuchen m	flan ; cake
Kugel f	ball ; scoop (of ice cream)
Kugelschreiber m	pen
kühl	cool
kühlen	to chill (wine, food)
Kühler m	radiator (of car)
Kühlschrank m	fridge
Kümmel m	caraway seed ; schnapps
Kunde (Kundin) m/f	customer ; client
Kunsthalle f	art gallery
Künstler(in) m/f	artist
künstlich	artificial ; man-made

Kupfer nt	copper
Kupplung f	clutch (of car)
Kurort m	spa
Kurs m	course ; exchange rate
Kurve f	curve ; corner ; turn
kurz	short ; brief
Kurz(zeit)parken nt	short-stay car park
Küste f	coast ; seaside
Küstenwache f	coastguard
Kutteln pl	tripe
Lachs m	salmon
Lack m	varnish
Laden m	shop ; store
Lakritze f	liquorice
Lamm nt	lamb
Lampe f	lamp
Land nt	country ; land
landen	to land (plane)
Landkarte f	map (of country)
Landschaft f	countryside
Landung f	landing (of plane)
Landwein m	table wine
lang	long
Länge f	length
Langlauf m	cross-country skiing
langsam	slow
Languste f	crayfish
Langzeitparken nt	long-stay car park
lassen	to let (allow)
Last f	load
Lastwagen m	truck

Lauch *m*	leek
laufen	to run
Laugenbrezel *f*	soft pretzel
laut	noisy ; loud(ly) ; aloud
läuten	to ring *(doorbell)*
Lautsprecher *m*	(loud)speaker
Lautstärke *f*	volume *(of sound)*
Lawine *f*	avalanche
Lawinengefahr *f*	danger of avalanches
Lebensgefahr *f*	danger
Lebensmittel *pl*	groceries
Leber *f*	liver
Leberkäse *m*	meat loaf
Leberknödel *m*	liver dumpling
Lebkuchen *m*	gingerbread
Lederwaren *pl*	leather goods
ledig	single *(not married)*
leer	empty ; flat *(battery)* ; blank
Leerlauf *m*	neutral *(gear)*
legen	to lay
leicht	light *(not heavy)* ; easy ; easily
Leid *nt*	grief
es tut mir leid	(I'm) sorry
leider	unfortunately
leihen	to rent *(car)* ; to lend
Leihgebühr *f*	rental
Leinen *nt*	linen *(cloth)*
leise	quietly ; soft ; faint
leiser stellen	to turn down *(volume)*
lernen	to learn
lesen	to read
letzte(r/s)	last ; final
Leuchtturm *m*	lighthouse
Leute *pl*	people

German	English
Licht nt	**light**
Licht anschalten	**switch on lights**
Lichtschalter m	**light switch**
liebenswürdig	**kind**
lieber	**rather**
Lied nt	**song**
Liegestuhl m	**deckchair**
Liegewagenplatz m	**couchette**
Lift m	**elevator ; ski lift**
Likör m	**liqueur**
Limburger m	**strong cheese**
Limonade f	**lemonade**
Limone f	**lime** (fruit)
Linie f	**line**
Linienflug m	**scheduled flight**
linke(r/s)	**left(-hand)**
links	**to the left ; on the left**
Linsen pl	**lentils**
Linsensuppe f	**lentil soup**
Linzertorte f	**latticed jam tart**
Lippe f	**lip**
Lippenstift m	**lipstick**
Liptauer m	**cream cheese with herbs** (Austria)
Liter m	**litre**
Loch nt	**hole**
lochen	**to punch** (ticket, etc.)
Loge f	**box** (in theatre)
Loipe f	**cross-country ski run**
Lorbeer m	**bayleaf**
los	**loose**
was ist los?	**what's wrong?**
Los nt	**lot** (at auction) **; ticket** (lottery)
lösen	**to buy** (ticket)
Luft f	**air**

Luftfilter m	air filter
Luftfracht f	air freight
Luftkissenfahrzeug nt	hovercraft
Luftmatratze f	air bed ; air mattress
Luftpost f	by air mail
Lunge f	lung
Luxus m	luxury
Lyoner f	veal sausage
machen	to make ; to do
Mädchen nt	girl
Magen m	stomach
Mais m	sweet corn
Maiskolben m	corn on the cob
Makrele f	mackerel
Malzbier nt	malt beer
man	one
Mandarine f	tangerine
Mandel f	almond (nut) ; tonsil
Mann m	man ; husband
Männer pl	men
männlich	masculine ; male
Marke f	brand (of product) ; token
Markt m	market
Marmelade f	jam
Marmor m	marble (material)
Maße pl	measurements
Medikament nt	drug ; medicine
Meer nt	sea
Meerrettich m	horseradish
Mehl nt	flour
Mehrwertsteuer f	value-added tax

meiste(r/s)	most
melden	to report *(tell about)*
Melone f	melon ; bowler hat
Messe f	fair *(commercial)* ; mass *(church)*
Metzgerei f	butcher's shop
Miesmuschel(n) f	mussel(s)
mieten	to hire ; to rent *(house, etc.)*
Mietgebühr f	rental *(amount)*
Milch f	milk
Mindest-	minimum
Mineralwasser nt	mineral water
Minute(n) f	minute(s)
Minze f	mint *(herb)*
Mirabelle(n) f	small yellow plum(s)
Mitglied nt	member
mitnehmen	to give a lift to
zum Mitnehmen	take-away *(food)*
Mittag m	midday
Mittagessen nt	lunch
Mitte f	middle
Mitteilung f	message
Mittel nt	means
ein Mittel gegen	a remedy for
Mittelmeer-	Mediterranean
mögen	to like
möglich	possible
Möhre(n) f	carrot(s)
Monat m	month
morgen	tomorrow
Morgen m	morning
Motor m	motor ; engine
Motorboot nt	motor boat
Motorrad nt	motorbike
München nt	Munich

Mund *m*	mouth
Münster *nt*	cathedral
Münze(n) *f*	coin(s)
Münzfernsprecher *m*	payphone
Muscheln *pl*	mussels
müssen	to have to
Mutter *f*	mother
MWST *f*	VAT
nach	after ; according to ; to
nach London gehen	to go to London
Nachmittag *m*	afternoon
nachmittags	p.m. ; in the afternoon
Nachname *m*	surname
Nachricht *f*	note *(letter)* ; message
Nachrichten *pl*	news
Nachspeise *f*	dessert
nächste(r/s)	next
Nacht *f*	night
über Nacht	overnight
Nachtleben *nt*	nightlife
Nachtlokal *nt*	night club
nachzahlen	to pay extra
nackt	nude ; naked ; bare
nahe	close *(near)*
Nähe *f*	proximity
in der Nähe	nearby
Name *m*	name ; surname
Nase *f*	nose
naß	wet
Natur-	natural
Nebel *m*	mist ; fog
neben	by *(next to)* ; beside

German	English
Neben-	**minor** (road)
nehmen	**to take** (remove, acquire)
nein	**no** (as answer)
nennen	**to quote** (price)
Netto-	**net** (income, price)
Netz nt	**net ; network**
neu	**new**
neueste(r/s)	**recent**
Neujahrstag m	**New Year's Day**
nicht	**not ; non-**
Nichtraucher(in) m/f	**non-smoker**
nichts	**nothing**
nie	**never**
Niederlande pl	**Netherlands**
Niedrigwasser nt	**low tide**
niemand	**no one**
Niere(n) f	**kidney(s)**
niesen	**to sneeze**
nirgends	**nowhere**
Nizzasalat m	**salad niçoise**
noch	**still** (up to this time) ; **yet**
Nockerl pl	**small dumplings**
Norden m	**north**
nördlich	**north ; northern**
Normal-	**standard** (size)
Normal(benzin) nt	**regular** (petrol)
Notausgang m	**emergency exit**
Notdienstapotheke f	**on-duty chemist**
Notfall m	**emergency**
notieren	**to make a note of**
nötig	**necessary**
Notruf m	**emergency number**
Notrufsäule f	**emergency telephone**

German	English
Notsignal *nt*	distress signal
notwendig	essential
nüchtern	sober
Nudeln *pl*	pasta ; noodles
Null *f*	nil ; zero ; nought
numerieren	to number
Nummer *f*	number ; act
nur	only
Nuß (Nüsse) *f*	nut(s)
ob	whether
oben	upstairs ; overhead ; this side up
Obst *nt*	fruit
Obstkuchen *m*	fruit tart
Obstsalat *m*	fruit salad
oder	or
offen	open
offene Weine	wine served by the glass
öffentlich	public
öffnen	to open ; to undo
Öffnungszeiten *pl*	hours of business
oft	often
ohne	without
Ohr(en) *nt*	ear(s)
Öl *nt*	oil
Ölwechsel *m*	oil change
Optiker(in) *m/f*	optician
Orangenmarmelade *f*	marmalade
Orangensaft *m*	orange juice
Ort *m*	place
an Ort und Stelle	on the spot
örtlich	local
Ortschaft *f*	village ; town

Ortsgespräch *nt*	local call
Ortszeit *f*	local time
Osten *m*	east
Ostermontag *m*	Easter Monday
Ostern *nt*	Easter
Österreich *nt*	Austria
österreichisch	Austrian
Ostersonntag *m*	Easter Sunday
östlich	eastern
Paar *nt*	pair ; couple *(persons)*
ein paar	a couple of *(a few)*
Paket *nt*	parcel ; packet
Pampelmuse(n) *f*	grapefruit(s)
paniert	coated with breadcrumbs
Panne *f*	breakdown *(of car)*
Papier(e) *nt*	paper(s)
Papiertaschentuch *nt*	tissue
Paprikaschote *f*	pepper *(capsicum)*
Papst *m*	pope
Parfümerie *f*	perfumery
parken	to park
Parkett *nt*	stalls *(in theatre)*
Parkscheibe *f*	parking disc
Parkschein *m*	parking ticket
Parkuhr *f*	parking meter
Parkverbot Ende	end of parking restrictions
Paß *m*	passport ; pass *(in mountains)*
Passagier *m*	passenger
Paßkontrolle *f*	passport control
Pastete *f*	pâté ; pie *(meat)*
Pauschaltarif *m*	flat-rate tariff

German	English
Pause *f*	pause ; break ; interval
Pellkartoffeln *pl*	potatoes boiled in their jackets
Pendelverkehr *m*	shuttle *(service)*
Pension *f*	boarding house
Personal *nt*	staff
Personalien *pl*	particulars
persönlich	personal(ly)
Petersilie *f*	parsley
Pfannkuchen *m*	pancake
Pfeffer *m*	pepper
Pfefferkuchen *m*	gingerbread
Pfefferminzlikör *m*	crème de menthe
Pfefferminztee *m*	mint tea
Pferderennen *nt*	horse-racing
Pfifferlinge *pl*	chanterelles
Pfirsich(e) *m*	peach(es)
Pflaster *nt*	plaster *(for wound)*
Pflaume(n) *f*	plum(s)
Pforte *f*	gate
Pfund *nt*	pound
Pier *m*	jetty
Pils/Pilsner *nt*	lager
Pilz(e) *m*	mushroom(s)
Piste *f*	runway ; ski run
planmäßig	scheduled
Platte *f*	plate ; dish ; record
Platz *m*	seat ; space ; square ; court
Plätzchen *nt*	biscuit(s)
Platzkarte *f*	seat reservation *(ticket)*
Plombe *f*	filling *(in tooth)*
Polizei *f*	police
Polizeiwache *f*	police station
Polizist(in) *m/f*	policeman(-woman)

Pommes frites *pl*	chips
Porree *m*	leek
Portion *f*	helping
Post *f*	post ; Post Office
Post-	postal
Postamt *nt*	post office
Postkarte *f*	postcard
postlagernd	poste restante
Postleitzahl *f*	postcode
praktisch	handy ; practical
Pralinen *pl*	chocolates
Präservativ *nt*	condom
Praxis *f*	doctor's surgery
Preis *m*	prize ; price
Preiselbeere(n) *f*	cranberry(-berries)
Prinzeßbohnen *pl*	French beans
Privatweg *m*	private way
pro	per
pro Stunde	per hour
pro Kopf	per person
pro Jahr	per annum
probieren	to taste ; to sample
prost!	cheers!
provisorisch	temporary
Prozent *nt*	per cent
prüfen	to check (oil, water, etc.)
Pulver *nt*	powder
Pulverkaffee *m*	instant coffee
pünktlich	on schedule (train) ; punctual
pur	straight (drink)
Pute *f*	turkey (hen)
Puter *m*	turkey (cock)

Qualität f	quality
Qualitätswein m	good quality wine
Qualle f	jellyfish
Quark m	soft curd cheese
Quarktasche f	curd cheese turnover
Quelle f	spring (of water) ; source
Quetschung f	bruise
Quittung f	receipt
Rabatt m	discount
Raclette nt	melted cheese and potatoes
Rad nt	wheel ; bicycle
Radfahrer(in) m/f	cyclist
Radlermaß f	shandy
Rand m	verge ; border ; edge
Randstein m	kerb
Rang m	circle (in theatre) ; rank
Rasen m	lawn
Rasierapparat m	shaver ; razor
Rasierklinge f	razor blade
Rasierschaum m	shaving foam
Rasierwasser nt	aftershave (lotion)
Rastplatz m	picnic area
Raststätte f	service area
Rathaus nt	town hall
rauchen	to smoke
Rauchen verboten	no smoking
Raucher(in) m/f	smoker (person)
Räucherlachs m	smoked salmon
Räucherplatte f	smoked fish/meat platter
Raum m	space (room)
Rebhuhn nt	partridge

rechnen	to calculate
Rechnung f	bill (account)
rechte(r/s)	right (not left)
rechts	to the right ; on the right
rechts abbiegen	to turn right
rechts fahren	keep right
Rechtsanwalt m	lawyer ; solicitor
Rechtsanwältin f	lawyer ; solicitor
reden	to speak
Reformhaus nt	health food shop
Regen m	rain
Regenmantel m	raincoat
Regenschirm m	umbrella
regnen	to rain
Rehfleisch nt	venison
Reich nt	empire
reif	ripe ; mature (cheese)
Reifen m	tyre
Reihe f	row
rein	pure
reinigen	to clean
Reinigung f	cleaner's ; dry-cleaner's
Reis m	rice
Reise f	trip (journey)
gute Reise!	have a good journey!
Reisebüro nt	travel agency
Reiseführer m	guidebook
Reisekrankheit f	travel sickness
reisen	to travel
Reisescheck m	traveller's cheque
Reiten nt	riding
Rennen nt	race (sport)
Rentner(in) m/f	pensioner
reparieren	to repair

reservieren	to book (seat)
Reservierung f	booking
Restgeld nt	change (money)
Rettungsboot nt	lifeboat
Rezept nt	prescription ; recipe
Rhabarber m	rhubarb
Rhein m	Rhine
Rheinwein m	Rhine wine
weißer Rheinwein	hock
richtig	correct ; right ; proper
Richtung f	direction
Riesling m	medium-dry white wine
Rinderbraten m	roast beef
Rindfleisch nt	beef
Ringstraße f	ring road
Rochen m	skate (fish)
Rock m	skirt
Roggenbrot nt	rye bread
roh	raw
Rollschuhe pl	roller skates
Rollstuhl m	wheelchair
Rolltreppe f	escalator
Röntgenaufnahme f	X-ray (photo)
Rosenmontag m	carnival (Mon. before Shrove Tues.)
Rosenkohl m	Brussels sprouts
Rosine(n) f	raisin(s)
Rost m	rust ; grill
Rostbraten m	roast
rosten	to rust
rostfrei	stainless (steel)
Rösti pl	grated roast potatoes
Röstkartoffeln pl	sauté potatoes
rot	red

Röteln *pl*	German measles
Rotkohl *m*	red cabbage
Rotwein *m*	red wine
Rübe *f*	turnip
Rückfahrkarte *f*	return ticket
Rückfahrt *f*	return journey
Rückkehr *f*	return *(going/returning)*
Rücklicht *nt*	rear light
Rucksack *m*	rucksack
Rückseite *f*	back *(reverse side)*
rückwärts	backwards
Rückwärtsgang *m*	reverse *(gear)*
Ruderboot *nt*	rowing boat
Rufnummer *f*	telephone number
Ruhe *f*	rest *(repose)* ; peace *(calm)*
Ruhe!	be quiet!
ruhig	calm ; quiet ; peaceful ; quietly
rund	round
Rundfahrt *f*	tour ; round trip
Rundreise *f*	round trip
Rundwanderweg *m*	circular trail for ramblers
Rutschbahn *f*	slide *(chute)*
rutschig	slippery
Saal *m*	hall *(room)*
Sache *f*	thing
Sachen *pl*	stuff *(things)* ; belongings
Sachertorte *f*	rich chocolate cake
Saft *m*	juice
sagen	to say ; to tell *(fact, news)*
Sahne *f*	cream
mit Sahne	with whipped cream
Saison *f*	season

Saitenwurst f	type of frankfurter sausage
Salat m	salad
Salatplatte f	salad (main dish)
Salbe f	ointment
Salbei m	sage (herb)
Salz nt	salt
salzig	salty
Salzkartoffeln pl	boiled potatoes
Salzstangen pl	pretzel sticks
Sardelle(n) f	anchovy (anchovies)
satt	full
Satz m	set (collection) ; sentence
sauber	clean
Sauerkraut nt	shredded pickled white cabbage
S-Bahn f	suburban railway
Schach nt	chess
Schaden m	damage
schädlich	harmful
Schaffner(in) m/f	conductor ; guard
Schallplatte f	record
Schaltiere pl	shellfish (on menu)
Schaltknüppel m	gear lever ; gearshift
scharf	hot (spicy) ; sharp
Schaschlik nt	(shish) kebab
schätzen	to value ; to estimate
Schaufenster nt	shop window
Schaum m	foam
Schaum-	sparkling (wine)
Schauspiel nt	play
Scheck m	cheque
Scheckbuch nt	cheque book
Scheckkarte f	cheque card
Schein(e) m	banknote(s)

scheinen	to shine (sun, etc.); to seem
Scheinwerfer m	headlight; floodlight; spotlight
Schellfisch m	haddock
Schere f	(pair of) scissors
Schi-	see **Ski**
schicken	to send
Schiff nt	ship
Schild nt	sign (notice)
Schinken m	ham
Schinkenhäger m	type of schnapps
Schinkenwurst f	ham sausage
Schirm m	umbrella; screen
Schlachterei f	butcher's shop
schlafen	to sleep
Schlafsack m	sleeping bag
Schlaftablette f	sleeping pill
Schlagsahne f	whipped cream
Schlange f	queue; snake
Schlauch m	hose; tube (of tyre)
Schlauchboot nt	dinghy (inflatable)
schlecht	bad; badly
Schlepplift m	ski tow
schließen	to shut
Schließfach nt	locker
Schlitten m	sleigh; sledge
Schlittschuh(e) m	skate(s)
Schloß nt	castle; lock (on door)
Schluß m	end
Schlüssel m	key
Schlußlichter pl	rear lights
schmecken	to taste
Schmerz m	pain; ache
Schmuck m	jewellery; decorations

Schnaps m	schnapps ; spirits
Schnecke f	snail
Schnee m	snow
Schneebrille f	snow goggles
Schneeketten pl	snow chains
Schneepflug m	snowplough
schneiden	to cut
schnell	fast
Schnell-	high-speed
Schnittlauch m	chives
Schnittwunde f	cut (wound)
Schnitzel nt	escalope
Scholle f	plaice
schön	lovely ; fine ; beautiful
Schorle f	wine and soda water mix
Schraubenschlüssel m	spanner
Schraubenzieher m	screwdriver
schreiben	to write
Schreibmaschine f	typewriter
schriftlich	in writing
Schritt m	pace ; step
Schritt fahren!	dead slow
Schuh(e) m	shoe(s)
Schuhgeschäft nt	shoeshop
Schuhputzmittel nt	shoe polish
Schuppen pl	scales (of fish) ; dandruff
Schutzimpfung f	vaccination
schwanger	pregnant
schwarz	black
Schwein nt	pig
Schweinebraten m	roast pork
Schweinefleisch nt	pork
Schweinekotelett nt	pork chop

Schweinshaxe f	knuckle of pork
Schweiß m	sweat
Schweiz f	Switzerland
schweizerisch	Swiss
Schwellung f	swelling
Schwenkkartoffeln pl	sauté potatoes
Schwester f	sister ; nurse ; nun
Schwierigkeit f	difficulty
Schwimmbad nt	swimming pool
schwimmen	to swim
Schwimmweste f	life jacket
See f	sea
See m	lake
seekrank	seasick
Seeteufel m	monkfish
Seezunge f	sole (fish)
Segel nt	sail
Segelboot nt	sailing boat
segeln	to sail
sehen	to see
Seife f	soap
Seifenpulver nt	soap powder
Seil nt	rope
Seilbahn f	cable railway ; funicular
sein	to be see GRAMMAR
seit	since
Seite f	page ; side
Seitenstraße f	side road ; side street
Seitenstreifen m	hard shoulder
Sekt m	sparkling wine
Selbstbedienung f	self-service
Sellerie f	celeriac
Semmelknödel m	bread dumpling

Senf m	mustard
servieren	to serve (food)
Servolenkung f	power-assisted steering
Sessellift m	chairlift
setzen	to place ; to put
sich setzen	to sit down
setzen Sie sich bitte	please take a seat
sicher	sure ; safe ; definite
Sicherheit f	safety
Sicherheitsgurt m	seat belt ; safety belt
Sicherung f	fuse
sie	she ; they
Sie	you (polite form)
Silber nt	silver
Silvester nt	New Year's Eve
Sitz m	seat
sitzen	to sit
Ski(er) m	ski(s)
Ski fahren	to ski
Skifahren nt	skiing
Skilehrer(in) m/f	ski instructor
Skilift m	ski lift
Skipaß m	ski pass
Skipiste f	ski run
Skistiefel m	ski boot(s)
sofort	at once ; immediately
Sommer m	summer
Sommerfahrplan m	summer railway timetable
Sonder-	special
Sonne f	sun
Sonnenbrand m	sunburn (painful)
Sonnenbrille f	sunglasses
Sonnenöl nt	suntan oil
Sonnenuntergang m	sunset

sonn- und feiertags	on Sundays and public holidays
sorgen für	to look after ; to take care of
Soße f	dressing (salad) ; sauce ; gravy
Spannung f	voltage
Spargel m	asparagus
Sparpreis m	economy fare
Spaß m	fun ; joke
spät	late
Spätvorstellung f	late show
Spaziergang m	stroll ; walk
Speck m	bacon
Speise f	dish ; food
Speiseeis nt	ice cream
Speisekarte f	menu
Speisequark m	curd cheese
Spezi nt	mixture of Coke and Fanta
Spiegel m	mirror
Spiegelei nt	fried egg
Spiel nt	pack (of cards) ; game
Spielbank f	casino
spielen	to gamble ; to play
Spielwarenladen m	toyshop
Spieß m	skewer
am Spieß	barbecued
Spinat m	spinach
Spirituosen pl	spirits (alcohol)
Spitze f	lace ; point (tip)
Sportartikel pl	sports equipment
Sprache f	speech ; language
Sprachführer m	phrase book
sprechen	to speak
Spritze f	injection
spülen	to flush the toilet ; to rinse

Spülmittel *nt*	washing-up liquid
Staatsangehörigkeit *f*	nationality
Stachelbeeren *pl*	gooseberries
Stadion *nt*	stadium
Stadt (Städte) *f*	town(s)
Stadtführung *f*	guided tour of the town
Stadtmitte *f*	city centre
Stadtplan *m*	map *(of town)*
Stadtzentrum *nt*	town centre
Stand *m*	stall ; taxi rank
ständig	permanent(ly) ; continuous(ly)
Stangensellerie *f*	celery
Starthilfekabel *pl*	jump leads
Station *f*	station ; stop ; ward
statt	instead of
stattfinden	to take place
Staudensellerie *f*	celery
Stechmücke *f*	mosquito ; gnat
Steckdose *f*	socket *(electrical)*
Stecker *m*	plug *(electric)*
stehen	to stand
steil	steep
Steinpilz *m*	type of wild mushroom
Stelle *f*	place ; point *(in space)*
stellen	to set *(alarm)* ; to put
stempeln	to stamp *(visa)*
Steppdecke *f*	quilt
Stern *m*	star
Steuer *f*	tax
Steuerung *f*	controls
Stich *m*	bite *(by insect)* ; stitch *(sewing)* ; sting
Stiefel *pl*	boots
Stil *m*	style

Stock *m*	cane *(walking stick)* ; stick ; floor
der erste Stock	the first floor
Stockwerk *nt*	storey
stören	to disturb *(interrupt)*
bitte nicht stören	do not disturb
stornieren	to cancel
Störung *f*	hold-up ; fault ; disorder *(medical)*
Stoßstange *f*	bumper *(on car)*
Stoßzeit *f*	rush hour
Strafe *f*	punishment ; fine
Strand *m*	shore *(of sea)* ; beach
Strandkorb *m*	wicker beach chair with a hood
Straße *f*	road ; street
Straßenkarte *f*	road map
Streifenkarte *f*	multiple journey travelcard
Streik *m*	strike *(industrial)*
Strom *m*	current ; power *(electricity)*
Stromanschluß *m*	electric points
Strümpfe *pl*	stockings
Strumpfhose *f*	tights
Stück *nt*	piece ; cut *(of meat)*
Stufe *f*	step *(stair)*
Stunde *f*	hour ; lesson
Sturzhelm *m*	crash helmet
Süden *m*	south
südlich	southern
Sultaninen *pl*	sultanas
Summe *f*	sum *(total amount)*
Super(benzin) *nt*	four-star petrol
Suppe *f*	soup
süß	sweet
Süßstoff *m*	sweetener
Süßwaren *pl*	confectionery
Szene *f*	scene

Tabak m	tobacco
Tabakladen m	tobacconist's (shop)
Tablette(n) f	tablet(s) ; pill(s)
Tachometer m	speedometer
Tafel f	table ; board ; bar of chocolate
Tafelwein m	table wine
Tag m	day
jeden Tag	every day
Tageskarte f	day ticket ; menu of the day
Tagespauschale f	daily unlimited rate (for rented car)
Tagessuppe f	soup of the day
täglich	daily
Tal nt	valley
Tankanzeige f	fuel gauge
Tanksäule f	petrol pump
Tankstelle f	filling station
Tanz m	dance
Tarif m	rate ; tariff
Taschenbuch nt	paperback
Taschenlampe f	torch
Taschenmesser nt	pocketknife
Taschentuch nt	handkerchief
Tasse f	cup
Taste drücken	push button
Tatar nt	steak tartare
Taube f	pigeon
Taxistand m	taxi rank
Tee m	tea
Teebeutel m	tea bag
Teil m	part
teilen	to divide ; to share
Teilkaskoversicherung f	third party, fire and theft
Telefonauskunft f	directory enquiries

Telefonbuch *nt*	telephone directory
Telefonkarte *f*	phonecard
Telefonnummer *f*	telephone number
Telefonverzeichnis *nt*	telephone directory
Teller *m*	plate
Tennisplatz *m*	tennis court
Termin *m*	date ; deadline ; appointment
Terrasse *f*	patio ; terrace *(of café)*
teuer	expensive
Theater *nt*	theatre ; fuss
Thunfisch *m*	tuna(-fish)
tief	deep ; low *(in pitch)*
Tier *nt*	animal
Tinte *f*	ink
Tintenfisch *m*	cuttlefish ; squid
Tisch *m*	table
Tischtennis *nt*	table tennis
Tischwein *m*	table wine
Toastbrot *nt*	sliced white bread for toasting
Toiletten *pl*	public conveniences
Toilettenpapier *nt*	toilet paper
Tollwut *f*	rabies
Tomate *f*	tomato
Tomatensaft *m*	tomato juice
Ton *m*	sound ; tone ; clay
Topfen *m*	curd cheese *(Austria)*
Töpferei *f*	pottery *(workshop)*
Tor *nt*	gate ; goal *(sport)*
Torte *f*	gâteau ; tart
tot	dead
Tourist(in) *m/f*	tourist
Touristenklasse *f*	economy class
tragbar	portable

trampen	to hitchhike
Trauben *pl*	grapes
treffen	to meet
Treppe *f*	flight of steps ; stairs
Tresor *m*	safe
Tretboot *nt*	pedalo
trinkbar	drinkable
trinken	to drink
Trinkgeld *nt*	**tip** *(money given)*
Trinkwasser *nt*	drinking water
trocken	dry
Trüffel *f*	truffle *(fungus)*
Truthahn *m*	turkey
tschüs	cheerio
Tuch *nt*	cloth ; scarf ; towel ; shawl
tun	to do ; to put
das tut nichts	that doesn't matter
Tür *f*	door
Turm *m*	tower

u.A.w.g.	RSVP
U-Bahn *f*	underground railway ; metro
Übelkeit *f*	sickness *(nausea)*
über	over ; above
über London fahren	to go via London
überfällig	overdue
überfüllt	crowded
übergeben	to hand over ; to present *(give)*
sich übergeben	to vomit
Übergewicht *nt*	excess baggage
Überholverbot *nt*	no overtaking
übernachten	to stay the night
Übernachtung *f*	overnight stay

überprüfen	to check
Übersetzung f	translation
überweisen	to transfer (money)
Überzelt nt	fly sheet
übrig	left over
Ufer nt	bank (of river) ; shore
Uhr f	clock ; watch
um 3 Uhr	at 3 o'clock
es ist 4 Uhr	it's 4 o'clock
um	around
um 4 Uhr	at 4 o'clock
umadressieren	to readdress
Umgebung f	surroundings ; neighbourhood
Umkleidekabine f	cubicle
umleiten	to divert ; to reroute
Umleitung f	diversion (traffic)
Umschlag m	envelope
umsteigen	to change
Umweg m	detour
Umwelt f	environment
unbegrenzt	unlimited
Unfall m	accident
ungefähr	approximate
ungefähr £10	about £10
Unglück nt	accident
ungültig	invalid
ungültig werden	to expire
unmöglich	impossible
unsicher	uncertain (fact)
unten	downstairs ; below
nach unten	downward(s) ; downstairs
unter	under(neath)
unterbrechen	to interrupt
untere(r/s)	lower ; bottom

Unterführung f	subway ; underpass *(for pedestrians)*
Unterkunft f	accommodation
unterschreiben	to sign
Unterschrift f	signature
Untersuchung f	test ; examination *(medical)*
unwohl	unwell
Urlaub m	leave ; holiday
auf Urlaub	on holiday ; on leave
Ursprungsland nt	country of origin
Vanilleeis nt	vanilla ice cream
Vater m	father
vegetarier(in) m/f	vegetarian *(person)*
vegetarisch	vegetarian
Ventil nt	valve
Venusmuschel(n) f	clam(s)
verbinden	to connect *(join)*
Verbindung f	service *(bus, etc.)* ; line *(telephone)*
verbleit	leaded
verboten	forbidden
Verbrennung f	burn
verbringen	to spend *(time)*
verderben	to go bad *(food)* ; to spoil
verdienen	to deserve ; to earn
verdorben	spoilt
Verein m	society *(club)*
vereinbaren	to agree upon
Vereinigtes König-reich nt	United Kingdom
Vereinigte Staaten (von Amerika) pl	United States (of America)
Verfallsdatum nt	expiry date ; eat-by date
Verfügung f	disposal

Vergangenheit *f*	past
vergessen	to forget
Vergnügen *nt*	enjoyment ; pleasure
viel Vergnügen!	have a good time!
Vergnügungspark *m*	amusement park
vergoldet	gold-plated
Vergrößerung *f*	enlargement
verheiratet	married
verhindern	to prevent
Verhütungsmittel *nt*	contraceptive
Verkauf *m*	sale
verkaufen	to sell
Verkäufer(in) *m/f*	sales assistant
Verkehr *m*	traffic
Verkehrsbüro *nt*	tourist information office
Verkehrspolizist(in) *m/f*	traffic warden
Verkehrszeichen *nt*	road sign
verkehrt	wrong
verkehrt herum	upside down
Verleih *m*	rental company ; hire company
Verletzung *f*	injury
verlobt	engaged *(betrothed)*
vermeiden	to avoid
vermieten	to rent
zu vermieten	to let
Vermittlung *f*	telephone exchange ; operator
Verrenkung *f*	sprain
verschieben	to postpone
verschreiben	to prescribe
versichern	to insure
Versicherung *f*	insurance
versilbert	silver-plated
Verspätung *f*	delay
verstehen	to understand

Vertrag m	contract
Verwandte(r) m/f	relative
verwenden	to use
Verzeihung!	sorry ; excuse me
verzollen	to declare (customs)
viel	much
viele	many
vielleicht	perhaps ; possibly
Viertel nt	quarter
Viertelstunde f	quarter of an hour
vierzehn	fourteen
vierzehn Tage	a fortnight
Visum nt	visa
Volkslied nt	folk song
Volkstanz m	folk dance
voll	full
Vollkornbrot nt	dark rye bread
Vollmilchschokolade f	milk chocolate
Vollpension f	full board
volltanken	to fill up (car)
von	from
vor	before
vor 4 Jahren	4 years ago
Voranzeige f	preview
voraus	ahead
im voraus	in advance
vorbei	past
Vorbestellung f	reservation
Vorder-	front
Vorderradantrieb m	front-wheel drive
Vorfahrt f	right of way (on road)
Vorfahrt achten	give way
vorgekocht	ready-cooked
vorher	before

Vorname *m*	first name
Vorschrift *f*	regulation *(rule)*
Vorsicht *f*	care ; caution
Vorspeise *f*	hors d'oeuvre
Vorstellung *f*	introduction ; performance
Vor- und Zuname *m*	first name and surname
Vorverkauf *m*	advance booking
Vorwahl(nummer) *f*	dialling code
Wacholder *m*	juniper
Wachsbohnen *pl*	butter beans
Wachtel *f*	quail
Wagen *m*	car ; carriage *(railway)*
Wahl *f*	choice ; election
wählen	to dial *(number)* ; to choose
Währung *f*	currency
Wald *m*	wood ; forest
Waldlehrpfad *m*	nature trail
Waldorfsalat *m*	Waldorf salad
Walnuß(-nüsse) *f*	walnut(s)
Wanderung *f*	hike
Wanderweg *m*	trail for ramblers
wann	when *(in questions)*
Waren *fpl*	goods
warm	warm
Warndreieck *nt*	warning triangle
Warnlichtanlage *f*	hazard warning lights
Warnung *f*	warning
Wartehalle *f*	lounge *(at airport)*
warten	to wait
waschbar	washable
Wäsche *f*	linen ; washing *(clothes)*

waschen	to wash
Waschmittel nt	detergent
Waschsalon m	launderette
Wasser nt	water
wasserdicht	waterproof
Wassermelone f	water melon
Watte f	cotton wool
Wechsel m	bureau de change
Wechselgeld nt	change
wechseln	to change ; to give change
Weckdienst m	early morning call
Wecker m	alarm (clock)
weder ... noch	neither ... nor
Weg m	path ; lane (in country)
weh tun	to ache ; to hurt
weiblich	female ; feminine
Weihnachten nt	Christmas
weil	because
Wein m	wine
Weinberg m	vineyard
Weinbrand m	brandy
Weinkeller m	wine cellar
Weinkraut nt	sauerkraut
Weinprobe f	wine-tasting
Weinstube f	wine tavern
Weintrauben pl	grapes
weiß	white
Weißwein m	white wine
Weißwurst f	veal sausage
weit	far ; loose (clothing)
weiter	farther ; further
Weizen m	wheat
welche(r/s)	which ; what ; which one

Wende f	U-turn (in car)
wenden	to turn
wenig	little
ein wenig	a little
wenn	if ; when (with present tense)
wer	who
werden	to become
Werk nt	plant (factory) ; work (of art)
werktags	on workdays
Wert m	value
Wertbrief m	registered letter
Wertgegenstände pl	valuables
Westen m	west
westlich	western
Wetter nt	weather
Wetterbericht m	weather forecast
wichtig	important
wie	like ; how
wieder	again
wiederholen	to repeat
wiegen	to weigh
Wien nt	Vienna
Wiener Schnitzel nt	veal escalope in breadcrumbs
Wiener Würstchen nt	frankfurter
Wiese f	lawn ; meadow
wieviel	how much
Wild nt	game (hunting) ; venison
Wildbraten m	roast venison
Wildgulasch nt	game stew
Wildleder nt	suede
willkommen	welcome
Windschutzscheibe f	windscreen
Winter m	winter

Winterreifen *pl*	**snow tyres**
wirksam	**effective** *(remedy, etc.)*
Wirt *m*	**landlord**
Wirtin *f*	**landlady**
Wirtschaft *f*	**pub ; inn**
wissen	**to know** *(fact)*
wo	**where**
Woche *f*	**week**
Wochenende *nt*	**weekend**
Wochentag *m*	**weekday**
wöchentlich	**weekly**
woher	**where ... from**
wohin	**where**
Wohnadresse *f*	**home address**
wohnen	**to stay ; to live**
Wohnmobil *nt*	**dormobile**
Wohnung *f*	**flat ; residence**
Wohnwagen *m*	**caravan**
wolkig	**cloudy**
Woll-	**woollen**
Wolldecke *f*	**blanket**
Wolle *f*	**wool**
wollen	**to want** *(wish for)*
Wörterbuch *nt*	**dictionary**
Wunde *f*	**wound** *(injury)*
Wurst *f*	**sausage**
Würstchen *nt*	**sausage** *(for boiling)* **; frankfurter**
würzig	**spicy**
Würzmischung *f*	**seasoning**
Yachthafen *m*	**marina**